C.99

CW01483728

POETRY NOW

NORTH WEST

1993

Edited by Pat Wilson

First published in Great Britain in 1993 by
POETRY NOW
4 Hythegate, Werrington,
Peterborough, PE4 7ZP

FOREWORD

Although we are a nation of poetry writers we are accused of not reading poetry and not buying poetry books: after many years of listening to the incessant gripes of poetry publishers, I can only assume that the books they publish, in general, are books that most people do not want to read.

Poetry should not be obscure, introverted, and as cryptic as a crossword puzzle: it is the poet's duty to reach out and embrace the world.

The world owes the poet nothing and we should not be expected to dig and delve into a rambling discourse searching for some inner meaning.

The reason we write poetry (and almost all of us do) is because we want to communicate: an ideal; an idea; or a specific feeling. Poetry is as essential in communication, as a letter; a radio; a telephone, and the main criteria for selecting the poems in this anthology is very simple: they communicate.

Faced with hundreds of poems and a limited amount of space the task of choosing the final poems is difficult and as editor one has to try to be as detached as possible - quite often editors can become a barrier in the writer-reader exchange - acting as go between, making the connection, not censoring because of personal taste.

In this volume around two hundred poems are presented to the reader for their enjoyment. The subject matter is as varied as the writers themselves, love, hate, war, peace, the seasons, etc.

The poetry is written on all levels; the simple and the complex both having their own appeal.

The success of this collection, and all previous Poetry Now anthologies, relies on the fact that there are as many individual readers as there are writers, and in the diversity of styles, subjects, and forms there really is something to please, excite, and hopefully, inspire everyone who reads the book.

This is a book that is a representative collection of poetry as it is being written today: POETRY NOW.

Contents

The Old Man of the Sea

There is an air
Of time and space
Etched within
The lines of your face.

Such a craggy face,
With tales to tell
Of sailing ships
And smuggling caves
Of excitement in
Those bygone days.

Oh, old man of the sea
Tell of your past
With stories of times
Which most interest me.

And I shall listen
In wonder, and earnest
In doing so,
Things will become
Much more clearer to me.

In the fact,
That you do
Love to tell,
Your stories of the sea.

You have had, I feel
Such a good past
Filled with lots of exciting times
And tales to last
You a lifetime though.

Oh yes, Old man of the sea
Please do tell your stories
To only me.

Baray

February Gale

The winds came howling down the night
And hurled themselves on the cankered poplar.
The stricken tree
Threshed and groaned as ailing limbs
Were torn from ancient trunk.

Trembling young ash trees
Bent before the baying blast
That snapped and snatched at brittle sticks
Then slung for crashing chase
Through their hurtling dark.

In full cry
They charged at the wall
Pounding bricks, worrying mortar,
Tugging and wrenching fixings of trellis.
Weakened by the onslaught
Timber and brick submitted
To be seized and flung
In frenzied fury.

Hour after hour the savaging continued
Till, cowed by dawn's pale face,
Whining they whimpered away
And morning light glistened
On snowdrops tears.

K Robinson

Cake

Whose silhouetted eyes above the bowl
Stir; stir; motion, now swift, now conflating dough
Filled with base elements, ingredients of soul.

Randomly, as predictive as leaves though
The ping, ping, ping from outer space fixed
A music in measured dances of oven time.

Our she god sings a verse of fractals mixed
To drop through a thermal space of mind
Dust stirred gases left from a billion past

Predicted not by Newton's silence nor Einstein's
Viscous pranks this cake exists regardless
Of recipes. This cake hisses iron and silicon

Water, fire and storms. This cake is earth;
Cosmos in chaos swirling in infinite forms

Measurably unmeasurable yet pulses heard
In universality from Feigenbaum
Before they are reborn iced
Frozen billions of fire at gas mark eight
Disbelief hurled into six dimensions spiced
And in the icing, the mathematic states
That God, a butterfly effect in China,
Is now chaotic hurricane in Rome.

John Hart

The Flower

My garden looked quite beautiful
With flowers here and there,
And even those who passed my gate
Would always stop and stare.

I watered it daily and hoed it well
And kept all the weeds at bay,
Then I noticed one morning a tiny shoot
So I tended it every day.

This tiny scrap of green plant life
Soon took and sprouted a shoot,
So I gave it lots of attention -
Not realising it was a spoof.

The days passed by, soon the shoot was a leaf
Bright green with a jagged edge,
And then I noticed several more
Had emerged beneath the hedge.

So I watered them all and cared for them
And they quickly began to grow,
In a couple of weeks I realised the truth
And wanted them all to go.

For I'd tended a savage 'flower'
Which doesn't care who it hurts,
Which smells neither sweet nor fragrant
And doesn't repay all my work.

I stared in dismay as I kept well away
From this plant with just leaves and no petals,
And I soon felt a fool as reality dawned -
For my plant was a stinging nettle!
Joyce M Lightfoot

Turning

As every Duce and Fuhrer must
The Czars and Caesars turned to dust.
Yet still the gunfire rakes the streets,
And Nations flags make winding sheets.
From children caught in crossfire webs
The blood of freedom flows, and ebbs.

While Maastricht fills mens minds with doubts
The burgeoned power of Brussels spouts,
With terroristic attitudes
And politicians platitudes,
Observing failing Gods of mammon,
Turkish Kurds and Danish Gammon.

America with pointed Gat
Looks on, complains and cavils at
The farmers subsidies in France.
While British miners find bechance
That they are being undermined,
Like Maggie, being Hesseltined.

Can cunning con men's conning maim
The Common markets common aim.
Doctrinal values bad and good
Be lost with aims misunderstood
And all the good men with the bad
Be fallen from Olympiad.

In nineteen hundred ninety one
Nobody thought it would be fun.
As Europe strives to rise anew
In nineteen hundred ninety two,
One wonders what is going to be
In nineteen hundred ninety three.
Cecil E Beach

Reflections of a Lost Dream

So, what now?
I sit and reflect,
A limp grip around my butterfly net,
Which is crumpled and broken down as now
The butterfly is gone,
And I am alone.
I had seen it from my window
Where it had hovered over the ledge below.
My God it was beautiful,
Red, yellow, green,
The colours of my dream.
And so, with my net I ran,
Away from home, me, anxious, excited man.
Though the butterfly hastened away
I still followed day by day,
Getting closer and closer.
This felt good,
Giving me a life, direction and laughter,
Making my legs run faster
At one with my dream. . . I was breathless,
Until my dream, the butterfly, rested peaceful,
And another net came down,
Just when I thought I had made it,
I was pushed into this bottomless pit,
Causing chaos, confusion, unhappiness. . .
The butterfly is gone
And I am alone.

Lee Brown

7

Beyond the Railway Track

All they see of the North
are pigeons in the back-yard.
Rubbish strewn by the railway line.
A burst and blown out umbrella
face down in the dirt.
A dreary reminder of damp days
when the sun doesn't shine.

Using the train as a swift camel
to cross the cultural desert
between South and the mist shrouded
mountains of Celtic Legend.

Beyond the railway track,
valleys a riot of colour.
Nature's glorious tapestry
of wild flower.
Abbey ghostly in the morning light
Markets alive with jostling crowds
have thrived and survived like the
cobbled street edging the picturesque
village green.
They lie unseen beyond the railway track

For the passenger with his refreshment
from the Buffet car.
Remains in his seat, and travels far,
in search of views breath-taking and
pleasing to the eye.
And all the wonders he lets pass by
beyond the railway track.

Freda Grieve

Desecration

Coronet of colours
Dethroned, Deselected, Endemic
Cut till they bled
Eviscerated.
Iridescent entrails glisten in midwinter
                                    sunshine
Bared for you to see
Alone.
Clawed victim stands gaping
Its beauty remains intact
Yet not eternal, for now
Fragments of an alternate reality
Encroach upon the sleeper
Shards of some other today refract
                                    incessantly

Perchance forever.

James R W Illingworth

A Bit of a Git

If pressed
He would admit to the existence
Of something other than logic could define
But wouldn't go so far
As to say it was important

Rather the opposite

Try to seize the intangible,
He would say
And it slips your grasp
Like a cosmic bar of soap

So he wouldn't waste his time
On what to him was imponderable

In so doing
He avoided life's most awkward questions
But missed out
On its greater possibilities.

Ieuan Phillips

Untitled

I sleep on an attar of roses.
I breathe through the petals of the world.
I dream. . .
I drift. . .
Love shrouds me in his velvet arms.
And the kiss.
The kiss of death.
Death is love; nothing to fear?
I am in love with an easeful death.
Blossoms trickle through his fingers
I am buried.
Buried in flowers.
Thorns decay. Only sleep prevails.
Love has died.
Love cannot die.
Dreams live on.
Whilst petals cry.
Weariness overcomes me.
Death overcomes me.
Love overcomes me.
But life will prevail.

Sarah Humphreys

Friday Night Fun

Spreading like a rash,
Slicks of smoke stain the sky
While at street corners
Men in white turbans gather and whisper:
The carnival has begun.

Friday night fun:
Living on the fringe of each moment,
Side-stepping cones of light
Which spill through cracks in open doors
As bodies flex around daggers of sound.

Weave a path to the ball of smoke
At the hub of the action;
It explodes the retina,
Framed around by liquid fire,
Hosing the mind clean of guilt.

Swords of water combat the flames,
Licking the metal torso
As the excitement thins away
And the crowds melt into the night,
Back to the pavement ghetto.

Alan Spencer

Wigan Heroes

Clean-aired Wigan - at what cost?
How many lives wasted and lost
underground?

No longer coal-dust, smoke and grime
pervade our town. Another time
makes no sound.

The time - our past. Buried, gone.
Yet silently it lingers on
all around.

Green hill. What secrets do you hold
within the depths of your vast cold
burial mound?

What horrors in your memory lie?
Explosions? Flooding? Left to die,
- never found?

Clean-aired Wigan - look with pride
upon the lives of those who died
heroes. Uncrowned.

Dorothy McDonald

My Red Admiral

Just as a butterfly flutters its way
Through my garden in summer,
So too will you wing your way
Through a brief season of my life.
Only to leave once the initial
Happiness of knowing is over.

Just as the butterfly brings joy
From its fleeting, free presence
So too will you bring hope,
Only to fade out
To someone else's garden.

Michelle Adamson

If I Should Lose You

If I should lose you, the rain will fall
And never cease to fall,
The skies of grey will shed their tears
And never cease at all,
The sunny days will all have gone
Darkness descending on earth,
And joy will turn to sadness
Crying 'what was this woman worth.'
And laughter will have turned its head
As myriads will mourn,
And night will embrace everything
And never bring the dawn.

A life so full of caring
Will be in peace at rest
And everyone will realise
They really knew the best.

A selfless, helping angel
That life can rarely bring.
A pleasure everlasting
That made the world to sing.
A joy to love, a joy to know,
All sweetness and all light,
Who lived a life of principle
Divorcing wrong from right,
And lived her life with dignity
Despite the endless pain
Until the tears of sadness
That brought the falling rain.
If I should lose you, the rain will fall
And never cease to fall.

Tony Sheldon

Perfection

Don't tell me that my looks aren't right,
my height,
my face,
my skin,
for God was my creator
and he filled the details in.

He wanted me the way I am,
he made these looks of mine,
a set of features quite unique
and perfect in design,

and if I'm lovely in God's eyes
then who are you to criticise?

Joanna Margaret Pridmore

16

The Owl

It hunts at night on silent wing
The mouse, the shrew, any small live thing.
It sits on high and surveys its realm
Always ready to swoop, to snatch, to overwhelm.
Not often seen, this silent killer
Perched on rock, tree, farm gate pillar;
We hear nothing but the dog doth growl,
Was it a tawny, a barn or a long eared owl?

D F Jones

Catch the Wind

Please wind collect me this cool Autumn day,
Carry me with you to lands far away.
Lift me on high over mountains and seas,
North lights, borealis, Alaska, the freeze.
Whisk me to Tangier, or West Zanzibar.
For deserts and jungles, Arab bazaars.
Drop me in oases, where wild orchids grow.
Drift me past high peaks, with cold frozen snow.
Sail me through valleys, virgin and green,
Through red sandstone canyons where no-one has been.
Down by small atolls, where men fish with spears.
The Tyrol, where climbers drink cold lager beers.
Tibet, where the Lama sees all and decrees.
Perhaps I will see him decree by degrees.
Take me to Athens or Italy's Rome,
For buildings and statues, Angelo's dome.
Hong Kong, the jewel, the light of the East.
Jade and mimosa, jasmine and tea.
Brazil, the Incas, Peruvian Andes,
Canadian lakes, log cabins and trees.
Sail me through night skies, velvety clear,
Where stars twinkle all night and music is near.
I've heard of soft music, sweet and serene.
White beaches and moonlight, seas calm and green.
I need to go now, with the sadness I've seen.
Hurry up wind, where on earth have you been.

Joseph Humphreys

Horsemen of the Night

When all the house is fast asleep
And frost has danced on twinkling feet and
Peter Pan has sprinkled stars
Along the Milky Way.
Ice castles gleam on hills afar
Their sentinel the northern star and
Tinsel streams glide softly by
Towards the southern cross.

They ride in twos in armour bright,
Those silent horsemen of the night.
To joust with stars on velvet black
Beneath the crescent moon.
Down paths of flint their horses prance, with
Pennants furled on silver lance, and
Burnished shields of crystal glass
They canter down the night.

Where shooting stars cascade the sky
The battlefields of Hades lie.
Young silver knights with diamond eye
Gallop to the fray.
They tilt at stars and whirl and wheel
And tilt again, bold men of steel.
Along the moonbeams silken paths
They joust the night away.

When all the stars have taken flight
And dawn is pushing back the night.
They canter back through Heaven's gate,
Those horsemen of the night.

David J Lavisher

Death of an Industry

They say thirty one pits will close,
And ninety thousand face the dole,
Fathers, sons, all cast out
to face a hopeless future,
Meanwhile heartless bureaucrats
are committing regicide,
As with a stroke, they sign away
the life of old King Coal.

Carole H Sexton

Metaphors of the Rose

I sniffed up the essence of a red red rose.
It is not true that the living simile is not there,
There is the fragrance, the headiness,
The touch of musk left by the male brush,
Then more dank and earthy down the stem,
And always, so wrapt with the ecstasy,
The first odours where . . .
'What do you think you are doing!' said a voice
Of one I thought a shepherdess, but she was too posh.
'That's not for the likes of you to touch in any way!'
Maybe she was the virgin Mary, she had the authority.
'That's for the bees knees, not for the likes of you!'
Whatever, she carried the mandate direct from nature
To banish such sniffers as me, for ever.

My love is like the red red rose.

David Derbyshire

Bluebells

Raised bell-shaped cups of sapphire petals droop
From slender stalks above broad opened leaves.
Whence rose those azure blooms near Winter's close?
Such early woodland heralds of young Spring!
Towards them scampers child from mother's hold
To gaze with gleeful grin on stalk-hoist gems
That peer through grass or cluster thick and wide
By dun or russet trunk of sleeping trees,
Whose boughs must longer wait for blossoms gay.
Pearl, silver snowdrop, topaz daffodil,
Rich sapphire bluebell, gold or ruby rose,
So sparkle jewels, Spring and Summer through.

John Buckle

Life's Waves

The breaking waves,
Upon our sands,
Briefly glisten.
Draw back, smoothing,
Removing previous
Imprints of existence.
Thus are we trapped,
Within these waves
To be reformed,
Smoothed, until form
Has faded into form.
And life exchanged
For death.

Bryce Flint

The Tapestry of Life

The tapestry of life is woven
In a web of joy and tears,
And the strength of this is proven
With the passing of the years.
Strands of love are golden glory
Threads of grey run in between.
Strands of black are sorrow's story,
Jealousy is purest green.
So the weaver tells his story
In a pattern bold and true.
Mingling with the golden glory
Is a streak of lovely blue.
Blue that speaks of eyes so tender,
Like the dawning of the day.
Woven in for love's surrender
With the pink of lovely May.
Sunset hues complete the weaving
Palest green and touch of gold.
Mellow shades of Autumn leaving
One life story softly told.

Florence Athersmith

So do you Love Me?

If I were lost, would you find me?
If I were thirsty, would you give me a drink?
If I were imprisoned, would you set me free?
If I were confused, would you help me think?

If I were starving, would you feed me?
If I were unhappy, would you make me smile?
If I were tired, would you help me sleep?
If I were lonely, would you stay awhile?

If I were in need, would you help me?
If I were dying, would you give me life?
If I were asleep, would you be my dream?
If I were burdened, would you take my strife?

If I were alone, would you be with me?
If I were a rose, would you bear my thorn?
If I were kidnapped, would you rescue me?
If I were leaving, would you be forlorn?

If I were hurt, would you heal me?
If I were weakened, would you make me strong?
If I were begging, would you hear my plea?
If I were singing, would you hear my song?

If I were crying, would you stop my tears?
If I were locked away, would you find the key?
If I were afraid, would you banish my fear?
Yes? So, you really do love me!

Linzi French

25

My Friend Xanatee

My friend is very strange.
My life I've had to rearrange.
He doesn't eat, and he doesn't sleep.
He doesn't even weep.

My friend is kind,
And also blind.
He has built-in radar.
He's trying to contact his home planet Sadar.

My friend is furry.
He talks very slurry.
I will miss him if he succeeds.
I'll miss his little, funny deeds.

He walks with suckers, on the wall.
He stands about four feet tall.
His hair's pink and blue,
And his skin has a purple hue.

My friend is not like me.
He's an alien you see.
No one knows he exists but me.
His name is Xanatee.

C L Jones

Seascape

The boom of the surf on the cold shore breaking,
The hiss of the undertow, pebbles raking,
The whisper of spray on the wave-crest waking,
   Tidal symphony, music of the sea.

The gleam of the white-winged gull steep wheeling,
The flash of gold from the lighthouse stealing,
Fitful clouds round the headland reeling,
   Cliff-top gallery, pictures of the sea.

The tang of seaweed in ship's wake shifting,
The smell of fish from the dockside drifting,
The waft of tar through beached nets sifting,
   Lure of the senses, opiates of the sea.

The bark of the seal at day's end mourning,
The scream of the kittiwake, predators warning,
The laugh of the dolphin, slow ships scorning,
   Wind-borne incantations, spells of the sea.

Startled crab out of harm's way gliding,
Mussel and winkle in rock-pool hiding,
Wispy prawns through the soft sand sliding,
   Bucket, spade and shrimp-net, childhood by the sea.

Pirate-ship and mermaid singing,
Smuggler in cavern dark, lantern swinging,
Sunken city with ghost-bell ringing,
   Old sea-dog's treasury, yarns of the sea.

Icebergs and coral reefs, hurricanes blowing,
Tempests and sea-mists, beacons glowing,
Sandbanks and rocky straits, cross-currents flowing,
   Echoes at new tide, the call of the sea.
Betty Everson

Hard Times

The intensity of his thoughts
Raged inside his mind,
His hopes,
Dreams, flashed before him.
A man, once so mighty,
So powerful,
Now just a shell
of his former self. As the
Coldness surrounds him,
Night falls
Like a black cloak.
His fatigue taking
Control.
Limply he rested against
The cold stone, now
His home, his
Bedraggled coat
Pulled tight.
Unconscious to his
Surroundings,
Visions in his mind,
Newly awoken,
Released him from his
Unbearable
Reality.

Pam Murtagh

Norma Jean

She burst onto the screen, like a queen from within a dream.
Hair of golden blonde, with a pout and a song.
With curves so rounded, and eyes so clear.
Our hearts always pounded, as she came near.

Norma Jean was here to stay, but the name had to go.
So she sat and thought of a new one,
and came up with Marilyn Monroe.

Baseball Joe was the first to know,
that he wanted to be with Ms Monroe.
He got wed and shared her bed.
But it was all a show, couldn't stand the thought
of Marilyn stealing the show.

She liked it hot, she liked life fast.
She knew with Joe it would not last.

A few men came into her life,
but none would have her as a wife.
Ms Monroe was a queen, to most men only a dream.

She shone like a diamond upon the screen,
Making sure she wouldn't end up a has-been.

Then along came Arthur, the playwright, Mr Miller.
Said one day the drink and drugs would kill her.
He took her as his wife, the last time in her life.
The last time she would be wed.
Years later found dead in her bed.

The queen of the silver screen, lay dead in her bed.
Fame had killed Marilyn, drugs had wrecked her head.

Too good to live, too young to die.
But the legend lives on, in our hearts and minds.
The Misfit of the silver screen,
will always be our golden queen.

M J P McManus

The Price of Slates

Slates on my house roof that keep out the rain,
where do you come from? Tell me again.
For centuries past those sediments have rested,
then quarried by Welshmen, health and nerves tested.
And what of the dust those miners inhaled?
That ravaged their lungs, which could not be veiled.
Medical men, I'm sure did their best,
to find herbal remedies just for the chest.
Of fourteen ingredients here's a description,
combined to make up a unique prescription.
Ipecacuanha, root of a shrub,
more potent than any frothy syllabub.
Lobelia, an expectorant and anti-spasmodic true,
with hyssop, pleurisy and scullcap mixed in a brew.
Capsicum, elecampane and many, many more,
black cohash and liquorice, watch the list soar.
Horehound, once a popular remedy for a cough,
while skunk cabbage is sure to cause some to scoff.
Aniseed, aromic pimpernella, known as weather glass,
with valerian and myrrh, what else could outclass?
For men who hacked slate, and hacked lungs unabated,
this special vegetable mixture was so formulated.
Now old slates from empty houses soon get stolen,
and builders look for any other substitution.
Tiles, stones and vinyls can make a modern roof,
so the human cost of slates is living proof.

Alfreda Flint

Ingleborough

Ingleborough; Yorkshire's wind swept crown.
Bleak and majestic with its constant frown.
Granite moorland; the curlew's call,
Gaping Gill and waterfall.
Footpath wending through beauty so bleak,
Leads me to the flattened peak.
Once the Icini dwelt thereon,
A trace of a thousand years gone.
Penyghent and Whernside stand near by,
Sentinels against the changing sky.
Summer's heat; Winter's chill,
Draw me to that constant hill.
Scrambling, scrambling over boulder and stone,
Satisfaction mine, and mine alone.
No one but the same as I,
Will understand the reason why.
In God's plan, and in Man's schemes,
man will climb to fulfil his dreams.

Barry Huntington

Feelings

As she looked up at me I could feel,
The despair in her heart, it was real.
She could not understand where he'd gone,
Why he'd left her alone for so long.
How do I tell her there's no love left now,
Tell me someone, please tell me how.
We had something special him and I,
How does it happen? How does love die?
But there it is nothing more to be said,
The feelings we had are now dead.

I said to her 'Sarah, listen and hear,
Your Daddy to you is still very dear.
But he is not coming home again tonight.
We'll lock up the doors and windows tight,
And learn together to do for ourselves,
Like hanging up wallpaper and nailing up shelves.
We must live without him you and I,
And we can do it if we really try.'
There is a life for us he said,
But the feelings we had are now dead.

We learned together, over the long years,
To live without him, to overcome fears.
And just as we settled and started to laugh,
He came to our door and asked to come back.
Now our hearts are in turmoil once more,
Remembering the day he walked out that door.
When our hearts were broken by his goodbye,
The night he left us and made us cry.
'Let me come back my darlings,' he said,
Now the feelings we had are no longer dead.

Linda Woodcock

33

Diabolic

Red tail lashing in the acid wind,
He stands majestic upon his hooves,
Surveying the realm of imminent pursuit.
His many headed hound straining to begin,
Sniffing the air for the smell of skin
Belonging to the one who sins.
He presses his hollow instrument to his lips,
Blows, cracks his serpentine whips,
And the game begins.
Relentless pursuit of an innocent;
Its soul to be torn from its body and claimed as a prize.
Hooves kick up hot dust and the chase is on.
His evil entourage chants and follows with gleeful fat faces and
Heartless hollows in their chests
Filled with the pleasure they like the best.
The hunted quivers under cover of building and bush,
Bristles with fear as the baying comes near,
Misted eyes and thumping heart, thinking only of the children left
By not surviving this brush with death.
This momentary introspection catches her off guard
And in a scarlet frenzy she is torn apart
And held aloft - the ragged, empty, tooth-torn shell
By apprentices clothed in the warm pinks of Hell.
Her blood smeared on the face of the young uninitiated,
They all return, their appetites sated,
Back to their cordless car phones,
Their driveways and wives' ways and six figure homes.
For the Devil and his followers there are no homes
They exist in eternal Hell;
But these huntsmen who chase foxes have fine places to dwell.

Wendy Bardsley

The Walk

I wandered lonely streets
wet and dark and empty
answering only my footsteps
leading me away
into the quiet night
of whispering sadness
nowhere to go
but solitude

James Abbott

Heartache

You're in my mind from dawn to dusk,
from sleeping to awaking,
In fact my Darling I'm with you
with every breath I'm taking.
I love you so my Darling,
that's why my heart is aching.
Our love my darling is so strong
that no-one else can sever,
so with God's grace and patience dear
we soon will be together . . . 'cause
when we are it is as though
a new world's in the making.
I love you so my Darling,
that's why my heart is aching.
So let us take each moment
and every stolen glance
to keep our love together . . . then
it's sure to enhance.

A Foxon

The Cat

The cat, uneasy, hunts away its night;
The pale mist clings; the grasses with shadows fill;
A twig crackles; and a darting vole
Moves the stillness to leave it yet more still
Beneath the tree, from the low grey light
Outwards, the garden creeps like a milky sea
And I can see against a still, old dead tree
The cat watching his prey in haste to flee.

Dora Doyle

The Fog

This morning, when I woke, the fog swirled grey
Like giant's breath, and hid the waking world.
The sound of cars was muffled, as the men,
Husbands and fathers, crawled their way to work.
No bird-song filled the air; but when the sun
Broke boldly through, a sudden starling flight
Swept past my window, scything through the mist,
And settled in the trees, which, early on,
The fog had kissed.

Jean O'Brien

The Gossip

Ee it's a while since a seed thi
I'd begun to think tha were dead
Tha were livin in Shaw wi yon Jimmy
Who thi Mam said were none reet in't yed.

He were workin ont dust cart fert council
The last time I seed thi, I know
He'd been t th' infirmary fer stitches
Cause he dropped a full bin on his toe.

How's thi Mother an Albert and yer Sam?
An I haven't seen Ethel fer weeks
Have they o hibernated fer winter?
Mind, it is pretty cowd now at neet.

D'you remember yon Harry fer Gas Street?
He ad a glass eye an a limp
He were always stood ont street corners
Mi Dad said he favoured a pimp

He broke int factory last Friday
An blew a big hole int safe
He were dead when they found im on Saturday
There were bits on him all overt place

Our Lizzie's gone livin in Owdham
She's getten hersell a rich chap
They've a bathroom wi o fancy trimmins
An a bell ont door - fancy that.

Well I reckon I'd better get home now
Th'owd chap ull be wantin his grub
Call an see us sometime and bring Albert
An we'll have a few jars down at pub.

V Harper

39

The Death of a Dream

A dream had been slaughtered.
Its head had been severed and
It lay dead in a pool of blood
It had burst out from boyish
Past, escaping the shackles of
Time. Dreams have habits of
Dying hard and when they are
Dead, die we.

I murdered this one. I with my
Bare hands, strangled and
Smothered it. A young boy's dream
It was. A dream about a motor-bike,
The kind of bike I used to like.
This little dream had come back
And awoke a green eyed infatuation
That had laid sleeping for a
Hundred thousand years. It was
Then that sense, that creeping
Pestilence planned its death.

'Think how dangerous a bike can be.'
'What about the wind and rain.'
Sense had hold of its head and
Shook it violently from side
To side. 'Can I afford it, and
The insurance too?'
Its head smashed and smashed
Against the wall, again and again
And again. It fell to the floor
Dead. Dead and *I had killed it.*

D T Noble

40

Early Morning
Newby Bridge in Cumbria

There is a place where peace is free,
Where salmon leap and laughter springs,
Where from the heart of all to see,
The wealth of nature clings,
There is a place where wild birds sing,
And crisp leaves dance on tree and road,
Where gleaming boulders smooth with time,
Enhance the river broad.

Moyra Wilding Rome

The Most Important Gift of All

A Picture of Grandad,
With a frame of a summer day at Allensford.
A picture of a friend who I can't see again,
With a frame of games we played.
A memory of birthdays,
With a picture of Christmas past.
The security of knowing my parents won't die for a long time,
With a promise of truth to the end.
But the thing I want most,
Is the promise of always having someone to help me in times of
 pain,
When I need them.
And the knowledge that my friends,
Are true friends forever,
With a sheet of sweet memories,
And a soft cloud to gently place my memories in.

Ailsa Westgarth (12)

42

Untitled

Pale child on a swing
whistles a haunting melody.
Aged memories long buried rekindle
painful thoughts in time.
Leaves swirl around the still playground
where once we played.

All that now remains,
is the ghost of my dearest friend Billy.

The tarmac rippled under a sticky summer sun.
Dogs barked at owners baited with sticks.
Lovers stroll hand in hand beside the lake,
whilst children shout and laugh
paddling in the cool crisp water.
Voices and laughter sounded all around the park.

Me and Billy played upon the swings.
So much fun trying to reach the sky.
Together we reached the top
as sunlight blinded us.
I glanced over, Billy was gone.
In the distance his poor limp body,
convulsed like a fish thrown upon land.

We were only having fun.

What lies before me now.
Flowers in front of the still lifeless swings,
where once we played.
A farewell to my dearest friend Billy.

Ian Shaw

A Flower's Lament

Why did you have to pick me? I was happy where I was,
I know the answer has to be because, because, because.
Because you wanted me inside to fill with fragrant air
To brighten up a dreary spot with all my floral flair.

Why could you not have left me in the garden where I grew?
Where I could rest at night and wake to early morning dew.
When I saw you coming down the path I surely knew
My days on earth were numbered as I felt you cut me through.

You gathered me with many friends and put me in your trug
And then you took me in your house and stood me in this jug.
Why did you have to place me where I could not see the sky?
Or feel the gentle rain or see a bee or butterfly.

As everyone passed by at first I got admiring stares
But now I'm withering away and no-one even cares
I know that any moment now (the prospect makes me weep)
You'll pick me up and throw me out upon the compost heap.

Oh what a way to end my days, I hang my head in shame
No longer recognizable no credit to my name.
Why could you not have left me beneath a sunlit sky
Where I could bloom contentedly until the day I die.

B Hampson

Arab Mare

Eyes set ablaze, nostrils aflare,
Mane and tail streaming, the glorious Arab
                                                      mare
The curves of her body as pure as the sun,
Arab prances forward, life has begun.
Her coat a sheet of beauty, her eyes stars
                                        in the skies,
Mane and tail a waterfall, as the Arab prances
                                              and flies
She rises on her hind feet, a picture of power,
She lets out her challenging cry from the peak
                                        of her tower
As her hooves touch the ground, her power
Flows through her in a strong moving tide,
Every inch of her body full of beauty and
                                              pride
Yet when she hears the voice of that girl,
She's transfixed to the spot, still and beautiful
                                        as a pearl
All her power is drained and overcome by love
                                        and trust
For the girl the Arab loves, and obey her she must.

Tanya Milne

Sonnet for Sally

Last night she was laughing, so wide awake
we thought that she would never close her eyes
and go to sleep. It was as if to make
her bed time everlasting. Lullabies
past midnight into restless early hours
and still we failed to recognise the signs;
she seemed so well, so bright, this child of ours,
that she could die had never crossed our minds.

Then this cold morning slapped us in the face
with chilling silence from her cot. Her eyes
not open, yet not fully closed; a kiss
of blue upon her lips spoke her goodbyes.
Eleven weeks, such little time, to know
that she was loved, before she had to go.

Margaret Parkinson

Untitled

Ironical, Invective, Satire.
Titled, 'Not old enough to retire.'
The last tragic scene, before the curtain falls;
lying, shattered, broken, made obsolete.
A story of thousands of men from the street.

Waiting around in the wings, as the grinding
down shudders a silence, that brings,
no encore.

There is no one left to read the script.
Only a mould of decay, it's a crypt.

Receivers wanted for talent audition where
The set on the stage is a run down vocation.
Special effects, on any sight, any location.
No curtain calls just a cry for motivation.

Mary Bell

The Angel with a Broken Wing

I looked up to the sky on a cold and winters night
I see a silhouette of an angel struggling in half flight.
She falls down near me, I open up my arms, to the falling Madonna
                                    of beauty and charm
A blistering light burns my eyes, as straight into my arms she did die.
I look down upon the ivory queen,
and I see a tear in her eye begin to gleam.
The clouds open up, a bright light shines through,
I look at other people, but they don't see as I do.
Again, I look down at her face, but now it is mine.
Now I realise, my guardian angel has come to tell me, this is my time.
Now I am light, a body I no longer feel,
I look down and see wings on my heels.
Floating up to the great gap in the sky,
with an angel in my arms and a tear in my eye.
The chorus of heaven begins to sing,
of the fallen angel with the broken wing.

Bohdan Kowalczuk

Dandelions

Don't pick the dandelions
Horrible weeds that grow wild,
These were my instructions
As I grew up as a child.

But I loved the dandelion clock
So,
I would pick them just to blow
Their fluffy little heads into the air,
One o'clock, two o'clock, three o'clock,
There!

Why are these yellow flowers maligned?
How is a flower or weed defined?
Have you seen them in profusion?
To me they form the same illusion
As daffodils, to Wordsworth's eye,
A golden field, a mellow sigh,
A sunburst fallen from the sky.

Sweet dandelion your beauty shows
You're worthy too of Wordsworth's prose,
I'll blow your clocks to spread your seeds
And fill this land with golden weeds.

Susan Craig Howard

Mother

Many are the times you've taken my hand.
Often when I couldn't understand
Tenderly giving me courage and hope.
Helping me when I couldn't cope.
Ever beside me when I needed you most.
Ready and willing whatever the cost.
Mothers are wonderful you will agree.
And my Mother meant all the world to me.

Mary Leech

First Letter

Can you write a story
That has no chapter?
Can you write a chapter
That has no paragraph?
Can you write a paragraph
That has no sentences?
Can you write a sentence
That has no words
Can you write a word
That has no letters?
Lost is your story
Without its first letter

E Foxall

Holiday Blues

Our last holiday was a corker,
Sun, sea and sickness in Majorca.
The topless dancing was a thrill,
But too much squid made me quite ill.

Mind you, my stomach was already used to the pain,
From what was loosely described as food on the plane.
I wish I'd stayed at home with mummy,
Was this the start of my Spanish tummy?

We went along to the Flamenco night,
All this hectic dancing was quite a sight.
I thought I'd be safe with a bit of paella,
That's probably what brought on my salmonella.

Then one night, stuck for something to do,
We took a carriage ride to a barbecue.
It was only after several courses,
I noticed our driver was missing one of his horses.

In our hotel the food was no better,
So I complained to our rep. in the form of a letter.
This was shortly before her strange suicide,
Face down in her soup - funny way to have died!

Ron Makin

To Muriel

If we could go again to Cumbria
And walk once more upon the Lakeland fells,
Then linger for a while in dappled woods
And gaze in wonder at a mist of purple bells;

If we could take the car through Borrowdale
And pause that we might bathe from Derwent's shore,
Then tread the lane to lonely Watendlath
And drag our feet through leaves of sycamore;

If we could seek the peace of Ashness Bridge;
Look northward to the heather-covered hills;
Sit pensive on the rocky parapet,
Or dip our feet in cooling mountain rills;

If we could search for scenes which artists love,
And once again within the bracken lie,
While watching sheep graze quietly near at hand;
Or hear a skylark in the cloudless sky;

Well then my love, that would be bliss indeed
And though I know it nevermore can be,
The knowledge that we shared those happy times,
Is now a source of joy and peace to me.

Ron Waywell

My Father

You hated me for all those years
not a flicker of love did I find,
Only the insatiable fear
of a man I called my father.

I cowered down like a frightened dog,
you were oh so cruel my father,
You gave me no love, nor understanding,
no time, no hope, no nothing.

But you're not to be feared,
only pitied instead,
for all the happiness
and love that you missed.

Now it's you who is frightened
with so little time,
and only a flicker of hope,
For a reprieve to put right
some things you regret
now that your death is in sight.

Maggie Walker

On these Rainy Nights

As I walk home stoned and broke
on these rainy nights
I think to myself. . .
why?
On these rainy nights
the world is so bleak,
there's nothing you can seek,
still I go on living,
breathing. . .
dying.

The wonderment of beauty and an affection once known,
someone with sight claimed that I'd reaped what I'd sown
but that doesn't make it any easier to live with.

Bleeding hearts put in winter's deep freeze for cold storage
even the July heat can't free it from this evil bondage
but that doesn't mean we have to give up trying.

Temperament fades as I lash out at my own body's desires
for each honest thought at least another ten are liars
still I go on trusting in my own instincts.

Could it all be but someone's cruel dream of comedy
surely I couldn't think up the most touching rhapsody
still I pen in my name under the slick prose.

John James Nisbet

Morning After a Row

I am not feeling feelingful today
My face is wearing a blank expression
Coils constrict my gut, my head is clamped
My spirit is down where no lights are shone.

My feet were cold last night in bed
My hair I felt receded further
Spots broke out near my lips and chin
The room was black with a laughterless dark.

My voice is captured by family taboos
The past declares I cannot speak
I am in the grip of a guilt imposed
I know I deserve your contemptuous smirk.

Duncan Fraser

Or is it Constantinople?

Istanbul beckons to me
from a picture on my wall.
Minarets, mists, myopic visions
of dark strangers.
Who cares if they're tall or handsome -
so long as they're strange.

Easy to please -
an air of the unfamiliar,
a sniff of spices,
a language I don't understand
and being lost
in a strange city

Maria Foster

Untitled

Up to my ankles in molten butter
I'd wade into your affections just for the hell of it
(bizarre as that may seem)
I'd love you after a hundred years
and a hundred babies of my mind
crawled on to paper to die or live.
Smooth is ironing, making love and
sunflower margarine.

Ursula Curwen

All in the Mind

There are times when you slide inside your mind
And wonder who you are
The way to be is too hard to see
And the journey seems so far

But pause a while and afford a smile
At least you're in the game
And all around who may look so sound
Are wonderin' just the same

So next time you slide inside your mind
Try not to look too deep
There's troubles there if you think too much
But don't worry now, they'll keep.

William J Glover

Lost Innocents

Scudding clouds
Hide planes in flight
Great iron birds
To join the fight

As bombs explode
The sergeant flares
The bullets fly
A searchlight glares

One last stand
A bugle calls
A soldier creeps
In flesh the crawls

Little lost boys
Come out to play
The game for each
May end today

D T F Clifton

Jays at Thurstaston

Three jays rested
in the shade,
at the turn of the day
in the summer wood,
motionless,
they watched us pass,
seemingly unaware
that we could
spot their plumage
of rufous and blue
and white and black
in the shady oaks,
though when we turned back
they knew they were wrong
and railed at each other
with raucous croaks.

Three jays screaming
through the trees,
telling us we were wrong
to intrude
on their statuesque beauty,
their white and black,
their rufous and blue,
and their solitude.

Geoff Fenwick

A Heart

I adore your eyes, so deep, so blue,
the kind a heart
could lose itself to.

Your honeyed lips, so sweet to kiss,
my heart aflame,
its beat amiss.

My heart, it breaks, with every glance,
yet when you smile
you make it dance.

I cannot hope, your love to hold -
to say these words
was much too bold.

Fool's words, my heart, it had to write,
kind words from you,
I prayed last night.

Say no - my heart will understand,
too faint to win
fair beauty's hand.

But yes from you would mean so much,
our hands to hold. . .
our hearts to touch.

Trevor Clibery

Untitled

When my long last flight is over
And my happy landings past
And my altimeter tells me
The crack-ups come at last
I'll head her nose for the ceiling
And give my crate the gun
I'll open her up and let her zoom
To the airport of the sun.
And that great God of flying men
Will smile at me sort of slow
As I stow my crate in the hanger
- Where all the fliers go
And he'll look at me and smile -

The almighty flying boss
Whose wings spread o'er the heavens'
From Orion to the cross.

S R Johnson

Grandmother's Tale

'Gran, tell us about when you were young!'
My darlings said to me.
'Can you remember the long ago
when you were as small as we?'
'Oh, yes! I recall the bye and bye
as clearly as yesterday
and see once again my mother smile
whilst watching me at play.
Sometimes to the Mersey we'd go to wave
my sailor dad off to sea.
I'd prod at the jellyfish floating near
as sea-birds were screeching at me!
When pea-souper fogs made our nostrils black
and ships sirens sounded at sea
'twas cosy to sit by a glowing fire
when indoors was the best place to be.
We feared God in Heaven and King George V
and respected our teachers at school.
We honoured our Mothers and obeyed our Dads
and lived under very strict rule.
Without video nasties or violent TV
there always seemed plenty to do.
We would work, play then pray before going to bed
I was every bit happy as you.
Much happened when I was a girl long ago,
I've so many memories in store.
Away now my darlings, it's past time for bed.
Next visit I'll tell you some more!'

Vivienne Joyce

The Noble Beast

Why do we kill
the noble beast -
because he is not like us -
because he cannot speak like us -
nor listen to our wise words.
No, he cannot paint like Van Gogh,
sing like Domingo,
nor dance like Nureyev;
but, he has a beauty -
unique to him alone,
and he has a fine spirit,
and a history
which goes far beyond -
the breadth of our imagination!
There is nothing to equal him!
Yet if Man has his way,
there will be nothing left of him!
All that remains,
will be the dying echo of his song -
resonating throughout
the world's oceans,
and The Universe -
til the end -
of Time.

Roberta Duxfield

A Loss

I could stand laughing in the sun,
I could lie back, the day's work done,
I could respond in carefree tone;
Or I could wait, and wait alone.

I could suffer through the night,
I could wait and see no light,
I could wage a hopeless fight.

I could love and feel no shame,
I too, could play this ageless game,
I could walk smiling through the rain;
Or I could wait, and wait in vain.

H C Taylor

Mordecai

I have to report my continued struggle with reality
I am winning (really)
forced into that inconvenient corner
that death drives us to
I am crippled by love
the fish and dinosaur
as Lowell observed on a good day
they get everywhere in silence
death has that quality
edging towards silence
you are in some other place
no crutch to me now
I envy you your wit and wisdom
while I, a creature of impulse
formed Rosalind Russell's lips on my face
you roared off to some other place
was that a mistake?

Andrea Lofthouse

67

The Sibling

Who is this lady, so tall and stately
With haughty manner and regal stature
Hair like fire and eyes like ice?
No-one suspects this cold disguise.

Who is this woman, warm and giving
Working hard to earn her living
Laughing, loving, warm and free?
Hiding her vulnerability.

I have seen her many faces,
Numerous as fields of daisies.
Know the truths deep down inside her
And know the happiness denied her.

Her complex personality is such,
Understanding her is much
Too difficult to contemplate,
So she arranges her own fate.

She lives in a world so different to ours.
She has strange thoughts, unusual powers.
Condemned as eccentric, she happens to be
Beloved beyond words, by her sister, me.

Shirley Baxter

Old Walls

New Country,
You've changed your outlook,
Your way of life,
Your name too,
Your laws and your uniforms.
It's all over the world,
A new map for the globe,
Another name for the history books,
A fresh leader to meet,
A new customer.

Do you think we have noticed your face?
Do we like what you do in your land?
Do we care as long as you buy from us?
Do you think we all understand?

Some live in the past.
Some know it won't last.
They won't even give you the chance
On the world's stage.

Whatever ignorance you see,
You're all now living free,
And you've a right to speak out
If you feel the need.

Voice your fears today,
They'll have to throw the curtain away,
And the rubble you'll clear
Are Old Walls.

Gordon Allen

Getting it Off my Chest

The homeless stare at an empty church
the clergy sit on a higher perch
the politician's answer is make more rules
never bother to find the cause.

Pollution the result of capitalists wealth
unconcerned for the world's health
an expendable commodity is how they think
our world is beginning to stink.

A future in heaven we're led to believe
hell on earth is what we achieve
conditioned to live in a time not here
conditioned to live in a future of fear.

V Wiggins

Love's Hive

Within my role of woman, Eve's Paragon, I,
May contemplate upon its loving cup,
Daydreaming, seek, and, sip, before I die,
To find the brink, o'er slopped, its youthdays sup. . .

Within my role, of yesteryears, and all,
Life's daydream maker, in the lack of age,
That brings like nectar's sticky dregs, and mirth,
Her hive uprooted, in its giving stage. . .

The bee that buzzes round, redundant haunt,
Plumpfull, of goodness, all for bounty's sake,
Finds, less than honey, from her busy jaunt,
To fly off, *piqued*, to die, for dying's sake. . .

Whilst there in dells, in misty, dewy, morn
Where sunlight melts the over supped blooms,
Late nurtured kin, midst green and mossy mass,
Oh, would they miss her? Would their hearts be torn?
Her lithesome friends, as bud, by bud, they pass. . .
Ah, no! The combs would fill, but just as soon. . .

So take not from them, merry, happy, souls,
Now in the haven, busy at their mill,
When flowers are scarce, but nature still is rife,
All poets, like bees, will work, 'till time stands still. . .

Kathleen Millington

A Cure

I am unhappy
She said.
I am insecure
She said.
It is this living together,
So they wed
Legitimising her insecurities,
And so
They lived unhappily ever after.

Janette Valentine

Lover Returns

I meet you at the station
where last week you left me
empty as a husk, for another.
Your dark eyes reach me
and unzip my stone case.
My armoured veins become
exquisite lace, a web
tender but impenetrable.
I have fear where joy trembles
under ridges of ice, numbed by
the long drag through grit.

No exile now
from your lascivious smile
which glitters like sunlight
through crushed ice. You think
your kiss and your sorries suffice
but you open left-luggage
to find a whorled seed:
hard, inscrutable,
not swelling for you.

Aspen

Mi Grandchilder

Today thi browt mi grandchilder
An' t' see 'em a wer' fain
Ther's little John wi' t' long pants on
An' t' babby a conna say 'er name

Little lad 'e 's none so bad
E'll play o bi 'is sel'
But fuss thi mak o' t' little un
Who's ruint a con tell

Thi stayed o day
An' a made ther' tae
It wer grand to see 'em ate
Yon little lad God bless 'im
'e fair mopped up 'is plate

Thi started clearin't table
But a towd 'em leave it be
Fer now a wanted owd o' t' child
An' t'diddle 'er on mi knee

An' then a played wi' little John
Till t' time for 'em t' go wom
Fain a wer' to see 'em cum
An fain when the'd o gone.

Edith Saynor

A Mixed Pot

Take a mixed pot, and stir it up,
Pick out the best, and smother with love,
Put one with another, and mould as one,
Leave to simmer until the heat has gone.

Hold for a moment a smile and a tear,
Be proud of what you are, be sure,
Wait for a while be quiet and still,
Keep the lid on what you've got, until -

Until hate and confusion and prejudice die,
Until understanding and acceptance lie side by side,
Until ignorance is truly a thing of the past,
Until you can be proud, to come out at last.

Eileen Lamb

Nancy Collecting Shells Along the Dunes

Nancy, collecting shells along the dunes,
Holds one to her ear, hears tunes
Of Man's salt ancestry. Watching I
Feel my heart move. Within, the cry
Of blood, that, like muscle, organ, bone,
Came in a wet zone
Somewhere, as either God gave life to earth,
Or Earth gave herself birth after birth after birth.

Tony White

Cat

Cat,
Slinking through an invisible jungle
There in the sunlit grass,
Oblivious hunts.
So we,
Creep through our world
Enacting ancient memories,
Our age-old bestialities
One against other
Long since outgrown.
Yet cat has grace and power;
So we,
And we should use ours fitly.

Jeremy Godwin

Our Countryside

A beautiful view from my window I see,
The river below and a blossoming tree.
Green fields are surrounded by hedge and stone wall,
The moor in the distance, a scene to enthral.
A landscape in winter with untrodden snow,
New life in the springtime when daffodils grow.
In summer, the garden with colours so bright,
The gold tints of autumn, a wonderful sight.
Our picturesque countryside, our pride and joy,
Is Britain's great treasure for all to enjoy.

Renée P Blackburn

Tangled Flowers
(Dedicated to Jean-Pierre)

A moment, a day, in a lifetime,
Fragile as butterfly wings;
We met for a while, and talked for a while,
Of many wondrous things.

An English rose in a foreign land,
Full blown, and past her prime!
We laughed for a while, and smiled for a while,
Just knowing another time!

A second, a minute, a lifetime,
Soft as a footfall in snow,
I knew you sometime, in another time,
Just knowing it had to be so!

A whisper, a glance, just seeing
Not strangers; but friends from the past,
Blossoms, tangled together,
Reunited together at last.

The past, the present, the future,
All gone in the wink of an eye;
In the breath of the wind, and the oceans roar,
In a look, a whisper, a sigh!

A moment, a day, in a lifetime,
All gone in a parting kiss;
Two flowers, entwined together,
A moment of fleeting bliss!

Jill Minion

Rainbow and Afterglow

Against the sky
An arc of vivid hues,
And, far below
The iridescent blues
Of April woods.
And fiery blossoms caught
In jewelled rain,
Celestially wrought.

In scented dusks
The fireflies plight their loves,
With dancing lamps
And softly singing doves.
While hunters sleep
The quiet owl prepares
For simple prey
His enigmatic snares.

Mary O'Brien

Wet September

The black Galloways loomed out of the murk
In the field across the lane.
From the high bank the cars on the road below
Seemed to float in their own spray
Like miniature Arks.
But no chance of a rainbow,
And no sign of Ararat among the fells,
Their tops hidden in cloud and mist.
No doves or ravens about this morning,
And no olive branches.
Only the goose and gander at the bottom of the garden
Under the pear and elder.

Caroline Ross

Cotton - King for a Day

The rattle and clatter of shuttles in looms,
Towering brick chimneys belching out fumes.
Teeming mill hands making a row,
The pulse of King Cotton, where are you now?

Row upon row of factory stacks,
Empty mill sheds stand back to back.
Blossoming towns dealt a harsh blow,
The pulse of King Cotton, where are you now?

Wealthy mill owners robbing the poor,
Mill hands struggle to keep the wolf from the door.
Union and management talks in full flow,
The pulse of King Cotton, where are you now?

Spinning and weaving now a spent force
We buy imported cloth as a matter of course.
Our own sheds now stand idle, row upon row,
The pulse of King Cotton, where are you now?

Cotton, a matter of national shame,
With owners and government sharing the blame.
For a thriving industry laid prematurely low,
The pulse of King Cotton, where are you now?

The shame of our mills, rank upon rank,
Empty, unused, windows all blank.
Or, demolished at last, dealt a death blow,
The pulse of King Cotton, where are you now?

The view as you stand atop of our hill
Shows empty sheds, mill after mill.
All of them closed by mis-management's blow,
The pulse of King Cotton, where are you now?

The pulse of King Cotton, where are you now?

John Catlin

83

Summer Time

When woods are flooded by a sea of blue,
bluebells and daisies too, thrown like
white and topaz charms across the fields
out stretching arms. Hawthorn smells and
cuckoo's trill echoing over trees and hills.
England in summer o what bliss, home comes
the wanderer for this.

Mavis Catlow

Whispers

'Listen,'
'Listen,'
A whispered voice ghosts past my mind.
Was it a memory?
Was it a thought?
A trick of the light!
Or a breath of wind,
Passing slowly through a half-open window.

The voice speaks again.
A bead of worry slips down my brow;
'Listen,' she says,
'Listen and you shall know.'
'Know what? What shall I know?'
'Everything,' she whispers.

The whisper is whisked away with the wind.
The memory eases to a moment of silence;
Dark, heavy, pressing silence.
It wraps itself around me;
It smothers me.
I run for a way out.

Finally,
'Listen, listen and you shall know. . .'
'Know what, what shall I know?'
She whispers, 'Everything. . .'

Anthony Kennie

The Gargoyle

The gargoyle
Has wings, of stone
He's alone and feeling
All those things
No mortal creature knows
The clothes, of dreams
He shows
As though to seem
To mean to see
Belief, in fantasy
Be fact
And acting out its part
The rain wears out his tears
With deadly animosity
Yet he succeeds to be
Totality
And passes, temporary, Man.

Norrie McKillop

My Lover

By the flowing waters edge
Beneath the hanging willow trees
Where sunlight kisses golden flowers
And dewdrops sparkle on the lawn,
My lover will be walking there
Amid the coloured tapestry
Of interwoven strands of green
Of yellow, violet and blue.
Bees drone round laden blossom white
And honeysuckle scents the air,
Yet perfect not the scene
Until my lover comes a walking there.
'Tis paradise, sweet paradise,
A heaven on earth beyond compare,
Yet all of it means little
Unless you my lover meet me there.

Jonathan Adams

Dancing with Angels

Floating, gliding amongst the fluffy clouds
Passing above the creature of the deep
All around a feeling of happiness
In the heavens, dancing with angels

Surrounded by patches of emeralds
Below an ocean of diamonds appear
All experienced with pure perfection
In the heavens, dancing with angels

Tranquillity emerges from within
Touching the souls of all who do see her
Drifting far, like a bird of paradise
In the heavens, dancing with angels.

Amanda Claire Currell

A Picture of Winter

When the warm colours which were autumn,
have all turned a paler shade,
and the giant oak reflects a steely grey.

When the skies have lost their blueness,
and the pine cones hang exposed,
and the warmness we once knew has gone away.

When the swallow's have all left us,
seeking out a warmer land,
and the dormouse it sleeps snug inside its nest.

When there's snowmen in the gardens,
with proud children by their side,
and proud parents judging which one is the best.

When icicles dangle down like fingers,
from the gutters of our roofs,
and the waters are all frozen on the lake.

When the shadows start to lengthen,
as each day comes to a close,
and the bones within our bodies start to ache.

When there's logs stacked on the fire,
and extra blankets on the bed,
and our woollens are all taken from the drawer.

When the kettles always boiling,
and hot broth sits on the stove,
and the draught excluders tight against the door.

When the north wind comes a howling,
bringing with it ice and sleet,
and Jack Frost begins to coat the window pane.

When our breath has all turned steamy,
and our fingers all turned white,
its then we know that winters here again.

Jael Dee

However

If there's one word that drives me to the end of my tether
Then it's that word of disappointment and rejection... *However*
It crops up everywhere, its so totally absurd
But never underestimate the power of this adverb
So why do I detest it, its uses are ample?
Well let me give a clue with the following example...

Thank you for your job application... *However*, at this present time...
Right Sir, you've finished your driving test... *However*, about that 'One-
                                                    Way' sign...
This is your Captain speaking, welcome aboard... *However*, due to fog...
Merry Christmas from all at number twenty-seven... *However*, if *your*
                                                    dog...
To-day will start warm, dry and sunny... *However*, by late afternoon...
We received your Insurance claim sir... *However*, under the heading of
                                                    'Sonic Boom...'
Yes, you *can* pay by credit card... *However*, due to the date of expiry...
The winner of the two-thirty is number six... *However*, after a steward's
                                                    enquiry...
We are pleased to offer you a loan Sir... *However*, there is a limit on what
                                                    we lend...
I was flattered by your poem and yes I *do* like you... *However*, only as a
                                                    friend...
We hope you enjoyed to-night's programme... *However*, next week's
                                                    edition...
Our Surveyor values your house at fifty-thousand... *However*, due to a
                                                    suspicion...
I can confirm your rights to property Sir... *However*, one of your family's
                                                    descendants...
Welcome to the hotel Senor... *However*, due to building amendments...

So now you see why this word always gives me the blues
Its because the words that follow... *However*... usually bring bad news!

Simon C Allison

Romantic Love

There was once a day, in May,
In my youth, when sunshine
Bathed the fields with a richness
of sweet delicacy.

And freshly cut grass in the park
Perfumed the air exquisitely;
And the sunset that night in May
Coloured pink and mauve and crimson
The whitewashed cottages of the village.

The air cooled as we walked across the bridge
of happiness - full of delight and the
Romantic love of springtime,
Quite unable to wait for old moon and the
Silver shafts of starlight.

Memories of the day, warm and tucked away
within us, lay secure in the bosom of our young lives,
No-one else allowed to touch them or sully
their precious secret place.

Our love:- spiritual and all-enveloping, moved towards
The inn with carpets-red, and hearth of fiery stone.
My hand, on your right hip, fell away to close
The portal'd door.

Alcohol warmed the very tips of toes and fingers,
Mateus Rosé' glinted in the firelight;
The shape of the bottle pleased my hand -
Like a breast.
Desire, and warmth, and all-consuming dreams.

Howard Procter

Abbreviated Life

'Less a poem and more a way of life.'

We live in a world where all is shortened,
Every action, every stage, every word, every page.

In a year AD we are born into a family
Which is usually RC or C of E;
And from early years at school we learn
RI, DS, PE, and history (both BC and AD)
To pass our CSE or GCE. 'O' level exams,
(And if grades are good enough 'A' levels too.)

We can then start work as PC's or SRN's;
Though some go to college to become a
BA, B ED, MA, PhD, or maybe all four.

At work we join unions such as NALGO and NUPE
And earn money for HP or to pay by PO
Or COD for everyone wants their cash ASAP.

To relax we listen to EP or LP, RCA records
Watch MGM films upon a TV screen,
Go to see plays by GBS or read book by DHL.

For holidays we tour the UK in MG's or VW's
At so many MPH; following the A506, M6 and
Other B roads to stay B and B for a day;
Or we fly by 707's or DC 10's at 1900 hrs
To the USA or perhaps just the IOM.

Our cars are looked after by the AA or RAC,
Our animals by the RSPCA or PDSA
Our health and welfare by the DHSS
And our education by the DES.

We vote for MP's, respect JP's
Admire OBE's but shun the AA's

Our yrs and mins tick away until we are OAP's,
Sadly to die at a future AD, but hopefully we'll RIP.
Surely life is short enough without abbreviation.

Sue Gerrard

Titanic

An April moon cast shadows,
A young 20th century clutches time,
A vast sleepy ocean lies waiting,
to lure a legend to its shrine.

A fearless laughter echoes,
A guilty pride reigns high,
Yet the fate, so tragic, in the winds,
lay furthest from their minds.

All laughter has now been swallowed,
Contented ocean, a sorrow immense,
Were the laughter and memories only borrowed?
Still the ocean breathes a deathly silence.

Claire Glover

Then

The snow was colder,
The sun was warmer
The clouds were whiter
The nights were lighter
The stars were brighter
When I was a kid.

The sand was browner
The sea was greener
The air was cleaner
The trees were taller
But I was smaller
When I was a kid.

The world was magic,
The games had seasons
With top and whip,
Hop, jump and skip.
Tensies with coloured balls
Against the playground walls,
Tossing up, skate and skid,
So much to do
When I was a kid.

Computers unheard of,
My books were well read.
I had to work out all my
Sums in my head.
I'm not saying it was perfect,
The things that I did,
But I'm glad it was *Then*
That I was a kid.

Doreen McKenzie

Penny Pilgrims

Nothing's as black as Nothing,
And yet there glows
A lit globe,
Lit blue from within.

Across her blue face
How many millions
Are dragged and driven
From continent to continent,
Packing planes and fleeing,
Frantic for life.
For light, for God's sake,
For life.
Before the dark will catch each one.

Each one.

Each one of us is carrying, each one
Is worshipping
Whatever God or vast machine
Is hauling
These Penny Pilgrims
From horror to hatred and back again.

The hunger for control
Makes the panic for life
Look like a dream.

The hunger for control
Makes the panic for life.

Peter Rigg

97

Kaleidoscope Colours

My thoughts-like kaleidoscope colours
Crash around my head.
I am the centre point,
And each way I turn,
The patterns change.
Each as unique and beautiful
As the last.
The intricate designs
Confuse and delight,
The colours and the light -
Intrigue me.
I close my eyes to concentrate -
Still I see the colours.
They circle more slowly now,
Each one quite clear.
The cobalt blue, cool as the sea,
The sparkling, gem-green emerald,
The rich gold warms me like the sun
And best of all-the ruby red
Wraps around me-like velvet.
I open my eyes,
Again the colours surround me;
They're cascading gently now.
They take me with them,
And I go willingly,
And peacefully. . .
I know not where.

Martine Marshallsay

Yellow Road Sarajevo

Sunrise through the dusty air.
A cracked blue sky.
Quiet shapes move into the light,
clutch precious goods, like hope
folded in flimsy tissue,
wait, nudged by stillness
thick with yesterday's embrace.
Hold onto silence,
brutal with yesterday's laughter.

A woman sits by the yellow road,
feels the hot sun squeeze the cracks in the sky.
Wipes away despair with the tip of her scarf.
By this road, long summers ago,
she held her lover close.
He is dead.
Lost with thousands more.
Pushed to separation and loneliness
by the killing that nobody wants.

She tastes the dust,
sweet with the sadness of memory.
A baby's smile, a child's touch,
the whisper of a moth in her lover's hair.
Two children dance on the yellow road to a crackling radio.
The buses come.
She will sit, wait for the dust to clear
and a sunrise that does not crack the sky.

Madeleine Keeffe

The Numbers Game

They're extensive on the bills that come,
but just one on the front door.
Complicated on bank accounts
HP's have several more.
Licenses and credit cards,
the post code and the phones,
library tickets, pay-slips and
long ones on the loans.

Without a host of numbers, I wouldn't get very far,
'I don't want your name Madam, just the number on your car,'
Don't forget the PIN's, National Insurance, P45
A jumble of figures that matter to survive.

The post brings all those lucky ones
to win! win! win!
A unique one for the wallhole - for banknotes,
a pile, so neat and very thin.
I've membership of all sorts
Unions, groups and clubs - it's hard
to remember - I'm even an agent - nothing exciting
just a catalogue card.

The fingers on the clock
the calendars digits date
and measure out my passing days
till St Peter's at the gate. (I hope)
But this is what I really dread
when I have finally gone -
He'll beckon - but will he call my name out
or a number? and - which one?

Eileen Bostock

Make - Believe

Walking silently over water, riding to castles in the sky
with knights in shining armour, as in days gone by,
where chocolate teddy bears play in the moonlights gleam
and candyfloss snowballs float on a river of cream.

Finding chocolate in your bath and ice cream in your hair
being free and happy, living in a world without a care
come with me down the milky way to my land of fantasy
where everyone is equal, and everyone is what they want to be.

Make-believe is for everyone, from four years old to ninety-four
it lets you do the things that you haven't done before
so if the world is getting you down, and your feeling low
remember to make-believe and all your blues will go.

Amanda Elizabeth Hague

Missing You

There is a time and place,
where gently harmonizing
thoughts, glowing with a warmth
that intensifies, to a burning
spiritual presence.

Here in perfect seclusion,
a timelessness, enslaving
ones reasoning, with the
presence of remembrance.

Cold reality,
breaks the illusion.

I thought or did I think?
for only the lonely knows,
with their saddened thoughts,
those who were bereaved
only yesterday.

Colin Rigby

Untitled

Machines are lying idle now,
In dark satanic mills.
Rust and dust have gathered there.
In those northern hills.

The looms have all shut down now,
No more weaving at all.
The 'Spinning Jenny' is resting,
Inside those industrious walls.

The mist surrounds the chimney tops,
At the break of day.
Streets are still and quiet now,
Shrouded by a sea of grey.

No more the sound of clogs pass by,
Upon the cobbled street.
Looms are silent and peaceful now,
No spinning dead-line to meet.

And now we have got progress,
To help us on our way.
So think about the future,
But spare a thought for yesterday.

Stephen Davenport

God is Enough

When the world seems dark and hopeless,
And the light is hard to find,
When the pathway's full of obstacles
And the way ahead is blind,
Just close your eyes, blot out the stress,
And think of the light within you:
God knows our needs, he sees our tears,
He knows our path is rough;
So when we've nothing left but God -
We'll find that God is enough.

Rhona Mitchell

Friar Tonight

Whilst prisoners pose with their po's at slopping out time,
How many of us lie snugly sinning in sleep?
Those naughty dreams beam in, committing crime
by mugging minds locked up in the cranial keep.

A village is pillaged by parsons snoring in smocks
as bobbies go battering baa-lambs on the bleat.
Judges snooze sentences on our bedside socks
that patiently wait to meet our morning feet.

There are nuns having fun with friars in the sky
flapping plastic macs as they wing their way from hell,
and there's Downing Street drowsing off opposition pie
as ticks click their way towards the waking bell.

Skateboarding Bishops collide with choirboys who
are playing punk on electric organs and
there are coffins creaking open by a pew
as alarm clocks move their menacing minute hand.

Psychiatrists say they rarely dream at all,
but I'll bet their couches are covered with luscious loons
all calling them crazy and driving them up the wall -
where they cling till the ring of the clock disperses the goons.

Now once awake, most po-faced people know
quite little or nothing about their nightly fun -
but do beware, take care when out you go -
for low flying friars might take you for a nun.

Robert Bakewell

Cathedral

More an outcrop of the stone it is built with
than the work of men; its silences

those of moorland, forest,
than of city backstreet.

At dusk grows windows of winter trees,
darkens to bellying crags,

black cave mouths, needles: the architecture
daylight veils. At midnight

the East face reaches for the moon.
Broods, an enclave of wilderness

among jostling complexes, a sanctuary
offering exile, exposure.

To enter is to mount a pinnacle of self;
to be crowned with anonymity.

Robert Bone

Who Am I?

Am I whoever I want to be
Or is there only one place for me?
If I learn all there is to know
Will I be me or just a mind of endless knowledge?
I cannot take the risk with my one life
To live it in ignorance.
Do I share my knowledge now or wait till I know it all?
Will I leave it too late and become just
Another idea on a familiar subject.
I want to be part of the process of
Extending human knowledge but am I willing to make
Sacrifices to get there?
If I make sacrifices will I become part of them and
Not me?
How can I ever be part of the process of extending
Human knowledge when I cannot answer
These simple questions.
Oh yes by the way,
Who Am I?

Alison Jane Pearson

The Storm

Deep within its ebony belly,
the pangs of hunger grumble.
With voracious appetite
resentful darkness swallows the light.
Random scars slice the sky with
razor-like precision.
Then, dense drops come drooling earthwards,
using unreasonable force to violate
the sun baked ground.
This secretion of digestive juices
is short lived.
No longer stunned by nature's menace,
its threat realised,
the earth resumes its measured breathing.

Brenda McLaughlin

Wans Tears Run Dry

Mine eyes thae canny shed a tear
sae strained wi bloodshot an wi fear
wi beggin bowl in haun I staun
an ask fae thae wa hae
anger beets inside ma breast
my eyes in sleep thae canna rest
wans brain in pain contempouous heid
canna mac yon sense
a queen on throne wit wisna suited
nine thousand million in her dooket
a land wits run by wimps o men
that surly cudnae truth a pen
while thae wit dinna hiv a shed
sleep in coffin cardboard bed
its thae wamac the rules in power
wit be response fir wan ither
pledges made have long gone sour
remember that election hour
jist tae ca ye in
fur its thae wa we lose we miss most
when its thae wit we hiv we shud care fir
fir its thaewa we lost wit cared more
for thae wit we hiv.

John Finnigen

The Night of the Fox

Midnight, stars and silence
Suddenly, there's movement in the bushes,
Closer, he comes into vision
He stops, lifts his head, sniffing,
Checking it's safe to continue.

At the garden's border,
In the barn, the hens huddle
Together: comforted by their closeness
Their scent comes to his nostrils.
He nears, his presence undetected.

He sees his chance, pounces
Through a half-open window.
Shrieking, the helpless hens scatter.
Though one would satisfy his hunger,
Something compels him to kill them all.

He leaves quickly, a hen
Held between his jaws
And vanishes back into the blackness,
Birds' bodies, blood, and feathers
Remain, carpeting the cabin floor.

Peter Burns

A Lie

I'd like to touch inside the world, and climb right in,
I'd like to commit a pure sin and see my sister cry -
A word, a word like die.
I'd like to raise a thousand hopes and drop them all,
A creature that is blind and deaf -
I'd like to see it fall.
A sky so black, that black is just a name
And life, if life at all, is just a losers game.
I'd like to see a lover without a love,
A hand, deformed, that will never fit a glove.
A child too young to understand -
I'd like to see it lost, in some far off land.
A tear, some bit of pain, a lonely sign -
I'd like to hear you weeping because you are not mine.
A dream, a nightmare, something quite insane -
I'd like to see you struggle, call my name.
A piece of wood, so hard and strong,
I'd like to see it crumble, a sad, sad song.
A misery, tormenting deep inside a soul,
I'd like to see you, locked away in some never-ending hole,
I'd like to hear you say you love me,
And I'd pretend I didn't know you -
And I'd pretend I'd never known you -
And I'd like to tell a lie.

Susan Anne Moore

Created Why?

Shalt it remain a mystery till I die,
and then shalt mans immortality prove to be,
a myth, a hoax, a fairy tale, a lie,
or visions most celestial shall I see.

Or when the earth was young.
With clouds of moisture hanging high,
until it cooled and fell as rain,
and formed our earth, our sea, our sky.

Shall I believe that midst this hot erruption,
upon which the vegetation slowly grew,
that step by step from this most foul corruption,
people evolved to grow like me and you.

And yet although my reason tells me no,
I still believe in God, the holy ghost and son,
if science and learning doth all this outgrow,
the victory of the grave 'er us is won.

C H Orford

Carnival Sound

My darling can yodel and sing like a bird.
All over Lido her sweet voice is heard
As she sets up Big Dipper, Hoopla and all
And twirls around on candyfloss stall.
In Bury aye o, in Bury aye o
Cheers and good health, lads,
In Bury aye o.

My darling can yodel and sing like a bird.
All over Rock her sweet voice is heard
As she leads the Parade coming thro' town
Skipping along to the Carnival Sound.
In Bury aye o, in Bury aye o
Cheers and good health, lads,
In Bury aye o.

If you should come to this part of the world
Wear a sombrero. Keep your toes curled.
Come to the carnival. Enjoy your stay.
Bring us success on a warm, sunny day!
In Bury aye o, in Bury aye o
Cheers and good health, lads,
In Bury aye o.

Chrissie Marley

113

Twelve Weeks

Loneliness is a single flower
Left in a naked room;
Emptiness is a sunny place
Where shadows harbour gloom.
Heartbreak is a film that clings
To eyes that cannot cry;
Hopelessness is the waste that lies
Where emotions have run dry.

Desolation is the garden where
Our children used to hide;
Misery is the silence left
Where laughter used to ride.
Forever is a hole to fill
With memories, like rain;
Minutes reflect the hours lost -
Time we'll never share again.

Pain is just a cactus plant
Surviving endless drought;
Torture is one, final plea
That can never be let out . . .
It took twelve years to build our love,
To watch it grow each day,
And yet it only took twelve weeks
To throw it all away.

Chris Firth

114

Untitled

I close my eyes
  And what do I see,

I see the person
  That I'd rather be.

A person calm
  And in control.

Content in body,
  At peace in soul.

The race of life
  Left far behind

A oneness in my heart
  And mind.

This perfect serenity
  All but a dream

It's how I'd be -
  Not how I seem!

The person there
  In front of you

Is always anxious
  About what to do,

Seeing others
  In a better light

Then turning inward
  With altered sight.

Ready to stand
   And absorb the blame;

A willingness
   To carry guilty's shame.

Trilby Little

In Memory

Joined by a common grief and seering pain.
A once proud city bows its head in shame.
Murder so foul, for one so young was slain.
Enlighten us dear Lord please tell us why
Sweet innocence and trust has had to die.

Believing in your mercy we will try
Until the last star falls down from the sky.
Love is the light to show this child the way
Give mercy to this tiny soul we pray,
Enfold him with your love and let him stay
Residing in your home till judgment day.

Mary Jones

Nine

The beauty is still there, the beauty that was once
All- consuming like fires of heaven drifted on liquor;
Still it stares to the snow-mirrored waste that is my mind.

The love is still there, once a law unbroken in the silence:
Starving in the night air these discords drown my sorrow.
Between the lines and the lies remains an unwashed passion.

The care is still there, as were many thoughts, once flickering,
Settling beast-like in the arms scarred by starling minutes:
Beneath the blinds your body slowly sips my love.

John H Booth

Easter Promises

Easter promises, to follow winter months - softly.
To tread carefully, less it shock the dormant earth.
The winter months have played their game and left us numb.
With not a single rose - to welcome Easter's birth.

Easter promises to woo gently, seeds hiding in the ground.
To bring forth cloudless skies and spring bouquets of flowers.
Hope renewed, will help us all feel carefree once again -
Awakened to the call of spring, caressed by Easter showers.

Easter promises a ray of hope, for weary souls who wait,
For better things - take heart! - they will be done.
Winter chills are all but over and summer days in view,
What lies ahead not matters now, that Easter promises to come.

Eve Davies

Two Maydays

I cannot estimate sharp numbers of bluebells bursting
each round of their garden springs up another ten or more

I can see growth movements of gold petals and wild daisies
closing under four clouds gripping gently

On the white on blue of the half-moon
they say is our sister - planet, lying dead beneath us

I have snatched dandelions from bees in wet hundreds
so that their spore will not sail wind to seed, and I have lit fires

Beside the cypress where collared doves refuse to tire
and leave eggs born still and cold as dawn

I have watched new life force out from October's pruning
and have read how many dead are still moving

Out of Iraq from what was no way
friendly fire

The moon has moved an inch across
paint stains upon the window pane.

They are reckoning the dead's number to be roughly
one fifth of a million.

George Owen

The Tree of Life

I plant this tree so you can think of me
When I am no longer here with you.
As it grows and branches out
You will know what life is about.
You will need the sun
You will need the rain
And stormy winds will bring you pain.
You must bend but never break
And you must keep going for my sake.
In the spring of your life when you are young and free
You will attract the butterfly and bee.
In summer when your blossoms show
The true meaning of life you will know.
In autumn days you will grow slow
And loose some of your natural glow.
In winter you will stand there, your branches bare
And many will pass who will not care.

Rose Morris

RIP

Why do birds fly
So high in the sky?
Why does light
Shine so bright?
Mum I'm hungry

Blond hair, blue eyes
Dark hair, Spanish brown eyes
Marks out of ten
What do you think Ben?
Sack tea we're on the pull.

Her face illuminates the night sky
No longer do I perceive the birds that fly.
Her silhouette the elixir of life
Ethereal beauty, soon to be my wife.

Buying a house
Now a spouse
Furnishing, bills
I could do with some pills
I'm hungry.

Average age, seventy five
I sense those years may have passed
In which one may thrive.
The children are growing
All too speedily
Time is passing all too readily
Perhaps now placated by a good meal.

Oh well
As the young may say, life's been swell
I have seen the birds fly
So high in the sky
And now
I visualize a light
Oh so brilliantly bright
Hello Mum, I'm hungry.

Tim March

A Lakeland Walk in May

See the leaves how green they are,
The scented woodland hue,
And everywhere the hedge and copse,
Is carpeted in blue.

Buttercups and daises,
Dot the fields with light and colour,
Blending shades of earth and sky,
Each one to the other.

Sweetly sings the meadow lark,
As she rises on the wing,
The cuckoo calls from far away,
Heralding the spring.

The fragrance of the blossom boughs,
Lingers on the breeze,
A myriad of bright wild flowers,
Amidst the lofty trees.

Splashing over rocks and stones,
The beck runs to the river,
The shimmering droplets catch the sun,
Cascading rainbows hither.

The mountains in the distance
Purple-edged against the sky,
And far across the tree-fringed lake
A flock of geese glide by.

A walk in May in England,
Still a green and pleasant land,
Where nature shares her bounty thus,
Despite the hand of man.
Margaret Martin

My Wilderness

I run - In which direction I go,
I do not know.
The wind is on my face,
the sun no longer shines upon me,
I am cold and tired but nobody can see.
I am alone in a wilderness of mechanical minds,
of men who are insensitive and blind.
They surround me in my loneliness,
but they cannot hear me cry.
'Oasis of love' Where are you?
Must I die?
But why?

Valerie Clegg

Colours of the Day

Dawn is a pale blue
Rising her head to the brand new day.
Golden days of sunshine
Springtime began today.

Moonlight streaming all over, you see.
The stars are winking down
Trees give us colour green and red,
But autumn leaves are brown.

Rivers of rolling water full of silver fish
Banks of flower's yellow, purple and white
A sunset red and orange,
The moon pulls the curtain night.

Linda Kilner

Computer Fever

So there I was on the home computer, playing this wicked game
when a familiar voice came up the stairs, calling out my name

Your dinner's ready, are you coming down?
and I felt my forehead start to frown

You'll know the score, my fellow buff
when you're into a game, one shout's enough

But seconds later, it was there again
and I'd just got the score past a thousand and ten

Alright, alright I shouted back
I'll be down in a minute, they're on the attack

They're starting to advance, I must concentrate
but back came the voice, that thing can wait

I won't be a second, I can't leave it now
and I felt the sweat run down my brow

Can't look away, can't put it on hold
If you don't come down its going to go cold

It's got control, this game is the winner
I guess I'll go down, and eat my dinner

Eric Scholes

Me and my Race

I can only watch with tears in my eyes
as the world around me wilts and dies
as the green belt slowly turns to grey
and the misused land erodes away.

And its me, you know, me and my race
who've forged ahead and made this place
a world of greed and dominance,
a world unsure of permanence.

And its me, you know, me and my race
who've forged ahead, torn down this place
to build a world of steel and brick
so you and I can get rich quick.

Still, industry made a man of me
and a billion pounds for my country
as the ozone fights the C.F.C.
and loses every time.

The greenhouse effect takes effect,
the Polar bear begins to sweat,
the professor says 'Don't panic, yet'!
as the oceans start to rise.

And its me, you know, me and my race
who've forged ahead and turned this place
into a dying toxic ball
that spins beneath a deadly pall.

With poisoned seas and littered plains,
acid lakes and acid rains
that fall like tears from blackened skies
onto a world that wilts and dies.

Ian Walker

Untitled

I came with the melting of the snow
On the high slopes sheltering the valley.
The purple, blue and yellow violets
Had just begun to turn
Their breeze-stirred petals to the sun.
Now they splash with iridescence
The grey stone pavement round the bronze
Statue of a troubadour playing his lute
In a fountain in an age-old font.

For many many years the old old-dame,
Who all in black now comes this way,
Has ventured out her home to see
One more spring paint the stony slopes
With flowers. Each year she brings a younger child
Of all her grand-kin grown that she may lean
Upon a shoulder to point out to them
The beauty of the blooms heralding
The summer still to come,
One they all know may be her last.

But there is no fear nor sorrow;
Only thankfulness the old eyes
Are strong to see and to enjoy
The loveliness that they behold.

Hiding here in the Pyrenees
Died the proscribed Albigenses
I sit near the church they built
Eight hundred years ago.

Racing clouds chase from the greystones
Brief touches of germinal sunlight
As the wooden slats of the roof
Lift in the circling wind.

No ghosts rise from the scattered graves
To tell of those they contain;
Only the cross askew the gate-top tells
They were Christian. It loosens still more
As the wind changes course.

T Hardy

Wine

Life seems so much clearer,
Through my alcoholic haze.
Sobriety an illusion,
Only wine can help erase.

If ever I should overdose,
On sanity and sense.
Two litres of the finest white,
Will help me recompense.

I used to live and love and try,
To lead an honest life.
Now I'm married to the bottle,
Less trouble than a wife.

Friends have said, things have to change,
Just pull yourself together,
But I have learnt the one true faith,
I'll worship wine forever.

Stuart Carey

132

The Children of Chernobyl

They are the children of Chernobyl
the children of the fire,
The children of the holocaust
the victims of desire.
With eyes as blue as azure seas
and smiles to warm the sun,
Those gentle children laughing, playing,
their lives hardly begun.
Gentle fingers touching,
caressing trees and flowers,
Dancing in the summer breeze,
to wile away the hours.
Their innocence beguiling,
their beauty of the stars,
Soon they will fly far away,
to Jupiter or Mars.
But those children of Chernobyl,
those children of desire,
Will take away a mothers tears,
enough to quench the holocaust,
THE FIRE!

Sarah James

133

The Cat

Furled furry and contented creature
Inhaling warm comforts from the homely hearth
Tranquil, cloistered, even tenored as the stillest lake
Wide eyes, enchanting, what secrets they must own, sphinx stare
Ears of parchment, triangled sentries
Consuming each microscopic sound that glides through the silence
This loving hand is drawn to you, caressing textured silk
Your thrumming body as the running stream, constant acknowledgement
Protecting innermost thoughts
Plushy paws hide polished claws
Lethal at the strike fleeting as an idea
Tongue pink, rhythmic perfection seeking, searching, cleaning
Oh Nocturnal traveller through the naked streets
Soundless a a shadow
Velvet athlete, legs pumping, silent jumping
Feline gatherings in untidy alleyways or black gardens
Plangent tones cry out in the still darkness
Holding court, action scurrying, scathing speed, settlement, peace
The pallid dawn approaches and with spirit and pride
You find your haven, duty done, some battles won
Returning triumphant, padding silently to your accustomed place
Reclining in still wisdom, although your sometimes scars suggest
Your Impenetrable gaze will say nothing
And I can go no further that to say I love you
And yet you know it already. . .

Hugh Connolly

134

No Hard Feelings

May the new love you've acquired
Please you to the Nth degree.
May he have what you desired
But you never found in me.

May your pills have coats of honey,
May your burdens all be light;
May your holidays be sunny,
And your Christmases be white.

May you never know a craving,
May your worries be remote;
And tomorrow when he's shaving,
May your lover cut his throat!

George Grady

The Prisoners

In this modern age of motor cars
Few people feel inclined
To don their coat and shut their door,
And leave their car behind.
To stretch their legs upon some moor
And hear the curlew's cry.
To drink the air like vintage wine
Beneath an open sky.

No more the family's Sunday stroll
Along our quiet roads.
Instead the gleaming metal jails
Whisk their human loads
Along at speeds that don't allow
Their prisoners to see
The passing scene, just forty miles
An hour and back for tea.

Maybe some pleasant Sabbath day
A prisoner will arise
Before his car, and steal away
To hear the wild birds cries
Out on the moor, and on that day
Maybe he'll feel reborn,
And vow to do it once again
Another Sunday morn.

Eric Johnson

Lundy

Beyond the Lowry puppets and the ice-cream,
The castles, the Frisbies and the dykes;
Far beyond the screams and demands and
Exiled into silence by time.
Stranded between two nations,
This fingertip of England protrudes
Like a growth on the tightrope horizon.

The name sounds like a curse.
An old Anglo-Saxon five-letter-word
To be uttered, when injured or thrown at an enemy,
Its sharp, cutting tail lethal to innocence.
Sullen and moody, it skulks in the mists
Ready to return for vengeance,
Counting the millenia as it crouches to pounce.

A primaeval rock with its green down,
Coughed from Bristol's throat and soothed by salt tongues;
Whose wrinkles and scars
Are etched by the same chisels that gouge us and
Is cradled by the sea,
Nursed by the swells and
Sleeps to the lullaby of the gulls.

Distant and grey this floating mountain
Riding the channel. The oldest ship in the world
Remembers her, as she still is,
Anchored to her bed by a submerged knuckle,
Nested by mysterious picture book birds
Whose cries tell the history of `
This comma in the sea.

William Weaver

The Snail

The body is soft and vulnerable.
How to protect it?
Grow a thicker skin.
The body is pliable.
How to shield its shape?
Grow another skin.
The layers are delicate
and a touch like a hammerblow.
How to stop the pain?
Create a shell.

From this it emerges cautiously -
but soon retires from insensitive eyes.
And the shell is heavy.
And movement comes slowly.
Slow is stupid - torment!

A white-hot probe draws the voiceless scream. . .

Dazed and tightly coiled within its shell
- only a surfeit of patience and kindness will persuade it
to trail the earth with silver threads again.

Charlotte Isabelle Brown

Endangered Species

Why do they harm,
Something so cute,
And so defenceless,
Perfectly mute.

Intelligent vessels,
Swim in the sea,
Leave them alone,
Let them be free.

They try to talk with,
Their cute squeaky voice,
Why do people kill them,
And show no remorse.

They could rule the world,
Because they are so clever,
To be as ignorant as man,
They could be never.

Riding majestically on,
The crest of a wave,
Diving deep into
A drowning grave.

Someone turn the tide,
And change people's thinking.
Stop these elegant mammals,
From surrealistic sinking.

They emit such love,
And joy to everyone,
Hurry up and save this,
Species before they are gone.

Man is only jealous,
To him they are a sin,
Try to spread the word,
And protect the Dolphin.

Julie Gleave

Ambition of Love

When I reach my ambition of life,
No matter whence that be,
You shall still be my mind's occupier
With the love you could not, would not, see.

For I have grown in strength of mind
To see you as you are.
And all I see is a sorry soul,
With his love at afar.

It is not love for which you aim
I see that now, indeed it's plain.
I only wish I'd seen it then,
When I'd freed emotions, now so dent.

For time is healing, so they say
And I submit my past of you.
Your self-indulgent, stubborn soul
No longer loved, no longer new.

Tracey A Murray

The View From Olympus

When the gods look down from Olympus
Sometimes they're close to mirth,
Watching man's stupid behaviour
And his talk of peace on earth.

When the gods look down from Olympus
Sometimes they're close to despair,
Seeing man's pollutants
On land and sea and air.

When the gods look down from Olympus
Eventually, they'll have had enough,
All life forms will be preserved
Except mankind - who'll vanish in a puff.

Val Gordon

She Said

The most painful thing
was heard,
words more bitter than the taste of a blade.

harsh serration,
sound from the lips of poison
twisted so that love became a noose.

Said with a cold glance,
emotionless and pale, the imperfections of thirty years now
in her bitterness more pronounced than ever;

she said the thing that she knew would eat
like a worm and kill peace. . . she said:
'Elizabeth thinks you don't love her anymore'!

In twilight and lies,
the words lodged in my mind and gnawed
as sanity fled

senseless through the tears that would stream into my hands,
run choking over bitten fingers raw,
and cry like a child for a child.

She could have told her the truth,
could have told her that
I love her so much, so much. . .

but she lets through inaction my precious child
learn to forget my love
as the poisonous mother

abuses with her silence,
molests with lies,
twists a happy love into the mirror of her own hatred. . .

Emma-Jane Arkady

The Mirror

He thought, as he gazed into the deep lifeless eyes;
Why did you enter into this unrepenting life.
Signed up, a bit of fun, for you can't escape.
Why did you beckon others to follow,
if you can't reconcile yourself, to love.

He raised his eyebrows, rippling his forehead till it hurt,
look now bastard, look now.
Drooping his head with shame, he clamped his eyes tight
holding back the flow of silent and tortured tears.
He knew were coming to haunt him, again.

Looking up through salt smarting eyes, he watched as the last drop formed;
slip silently from his nose, over his stiff upper lip:
and fell to the lost oblivion for which he longed.
The mirror had no sympathy, for it had seen it all before,
many times before.

Theodore Halsall

Addictions

Black coffee
Cigarettes
Nicotine
No regrets.

Stimulants
Come my way
Caffeine, fags
Here to stay.

Take a sip
Bitter taste
Take a drag
Problems faced.

Can't face life
Without fags
Matters not
My friend nags.

Caffeine drink
Keeps me sane
Nicotine
Does the same.

Feeling good
Relaxed now
Addictions
Yes and how!

Dianne Croskell

The Penetrators

Beneath the soft blanketed virgin bed,
Tentative tentacles furrowed,
Through fungus fossiled foliage,
Into dark chasms of the primeval past,
And tranquil fluids stirred.

Furious white horse warriors fought,
Smashing, intrusive hollowed legs,
With thunderous spluttering sprays,
And the mist shrouded giant shuddered.

Huge pipes clattered and clanged,
Red limbed roustabouts toiled,
On the mud splattered, wind-swept drill floor,
And mother natures, bilious, gushing gasp was heard.

Howling hurricane winds screamed,
As back bursting clouds,
Fanned, the flame flattened flare,
And wet suit workers fled for cover.

Prevailing winds abated, stormy seas calmed.
Guardians no more.
The great capped well was sealed.

John Fagan

The King of Suburbia

Insomnia peeps through the weary pane. As the
darkest hour awaits the pastel dawn. All serene
and still as sparklers blink and shower incandescent

signs on razor-sharp horizoned peaks. And space lasers
stab deep and chill into the svelte urbane savanna
cramped within my mortared, mortgaged redbrick wilderness.

A flash announces sharp, but hushed, a predator
(sly and shy) secreted deep within the silent dark
chrysanthemums and F1 hybrid Brompton stocks.

Staccato eyes refract and pierce the cold black void,
probing like the nightclub stroboscope in a funky
disco hunting scene. A sudden streak. Abrupt. Stops!

A statuesque situ. Then a cool-deliberate-motioned
stalk sees a punctuated paw, slowly prick out
it's precision path. Slow, slow, not quick, slow.

Exposed. Spotlighted splendour, transparently
shrouded in dormant quick-silvered star quality.
The supple spine is arched, the hackled skull held high,

the hypnotic tail sways with a steady hearted
Afro beat and right in the middle of my back lawn;
filthy nature fouls up the pastel dawn.

Douglas F Clink

Birdy

Like a frightened bird she sits,
flightless;
Corner territory precariously held,
Life a straining pulse.
If she lives little birds will die;
But for now she suffers, as the future
Tilts randomly
From life
To death
And back again.

Stephen Michael Brie

The Hen Party

Seven bridesmaids stalk the night,
Looking for fun and fiancés.
Disco debs anticipate sweet success,
Or happy-ever-after, as they hit the bright lights.

Seven bridesmaids dance with their handbags,
Smiles wither wistfully when no-one notices.
Willing eyes watch gorgeous men
Watch svelte blondes walk away.

Bridesmaids don't do that - they kiss a lot,
And sometimes screw around,
But, hey, who cares when you're
Still looking for a husband?

A final flirtation ripples rumours
In the minds of those who stand back
And make jealous judgements -
Bridesmaids talk dirty, talk trouble.

False flashing eyes photocopy passion
For tomorrow's hottest gossip.
They pity one who sleeps softly in ignorance,
Consider consolation their rightful prize.

Spurned, bored bridesmaids go home early
To cold empty bedsits. Sleep around
Femmes fatales in your flannelette and socks
And dream of white satin and lace.

Jane Clarkson

Dead Moth

Wild Gypsy moth
You fluttered and soared,
Delicate wings in air.

How did you stay aloft,
How did you stay so soft,
When the world showed
It didn't care.

You lie on ground,
No more beauty found.
Still do you hold mystery
In your sweet wing.

Dust on my fingers,
From your soft head,
No more pain,
No more dread.

Farewell little moth,
Span so brief.
Your epitaph I write.

A moth is a moth,
Steel is steel.
Choose which you may.
Mans madness and all he brings,
Or moth on silent free wing.
I choose thee.

Maureen Given

151

Untitled

Tonight the moon stage-manages
Its own choreography commanding of the clouds
A turbulent symphony
The lolloping and leggy breeze
Of the cool midnight sky
Takes on a violet-stained disguise
As if to entertain those of us
Not occupied in dreams
Its shapes describe no animal thought or insect
Flutter
No they wander
Intermingling cob-webby surfaces of soundlessness
Play kiss-catch
Under the protective eye
Of mother ozone
Dance gaily hippety hop
As if under the influence of the laws of nature
Thermodynamics
The mischief maker
Peeping out from behind this tittering mass of fun
Affects us all as we watch
Sucks our thoughts out to meet its awesome mesmerising gaze
Betrays us all to its captor
The living Earth
Upon which we live the wretched race
And weeps
Guilt ridden at the end of its patrol
For it will miss me
And me alone
For tonight it was I who fell in love with its sky
This very private performance was for *Me*
To see the moon die.

Hertzan Chimera

152

Life a Movement

Blossom where you're planted,
From a peaceful base,
Outwards ever outwards,
Until the arms embrace.

Encircling the newborn,
Enguarding the old,
Enjoining all together,
Embracing all the fold.

Evelyn Reed

Cry

Redundant, forgotten
Its tough at the bottom
This pit where I sit
This feeling like shit.

Drifting compassion
This wavering fashion
These enemies were work fellows
Ten minutes ago.

Fingers and bones
There are no rolling stones
Debris is gathered
Work ethics in tatters.

One million
Two million
Three million
And one.
He goes, you stay
You're gone, she stays.

Count my pennies
And count my fate
Plan for tomorrow?
Cry for today.

Martin Wardley

Dreamland

Dear child,
where have you gone tonight?
Your tiny head so peaceful lies.
To another world
Unknown to us
upon the clouds where angels
gently puff you
round the heavens?
To play with the moon
so big and yellow
and touch the stars
watching them sparkle
in the blackest night,
then slide down moonbeams
and shake the stardust
from your curly hair?
Do they let you climb the stairway
up to heaven
and peep through tinselled curtains
to kiss the Holy Babe?

This smile.
If only I could share its secret.
It must be a happy place
to lighten such a tiny face.

M I Turner

My City

Where is the city I knew so well.
There on the outskirts I used to dwell.
Victorian buildings soot covered and black.
Oh' how I wish the clock would turn back.

Pennies would take you a ride into Town.
Where you could have seats upstairs or down.
Conductors would shout out stops here and there.
Never forgetting though collecting your fare.

Whit Monday was fun and Whit Friday too.
With Brass Bands and Pipe Bands and policemen in blue.
'The Children of Mary' with banners held high.
And gaily dressed children sedately walked by.
Policemen on horses brought up the rear
Saving a smile for our final cheer.

I look with regret on new buildings high
Away in the distance flats reach to the sky.
I see from afar the windows are small
Not like the Bay windows I fondly recall.

I wonder if they know the people next door
Or just how many families live on the same floor.
Isolation, loneliness, linked sometimes with fear.
And there's no one to comfort that hastily wiped tear.

Friendships are lost, folk moved away.
Areas all flattened so no one can stay.
I sadly question the resentment I hold.
The answer is plainly that I'm growing *Old*.

Sheila Rowark

Her Bluebell Wood

How choice! a memory revived,
Once very dear, but now not tied.
Some instant thing will call to mind
A pleasant thing of human kind,
Just like a bell that rings,
Thought rushing through, determining.

Who was it? When and where, in years ago, so long?
We met to walk and talk, and wandered, so I thought!
A shaded lane, quiet and long.
She took me to the gate and then I saw, so grand a scene
As any I had ever seen,
A wondrous view,
So very blue.

There seemed a tree of every hue,
A carpet too, of bluebells new.

I want so much a photo mind
To treasure it with paint and brush
Or print it in my memory, thus.

'Tis memory indeed, could I retrace
Those quickened steps and walk intent
To see again that beauty, bluebell wood.

She'll not be there, or anywhere
I know, or hope for, unaware!

Alfred Shute

It's Raining and Dark Now

You always said you'd give me the world one day
you never did, did you?

But that night
when you stopped the hedges from blurring
and gave the rabbits and foxes a better chance at survival
you took my hand and we hopped and skipped
through the dry and ready cornfield

Oh midsummer, midsummer

To Jacksons pond you took me
your teeth lighting our way
a wry and arrogant smile

we sat amongst the bulrushes kissing
and you said that we should play a game of Moses
your hands then disappeared into the frying pan waters and
slowly, with sweat on your brow, you pulled out the moon

Oh midsummer, midsummer

I said in confusion that it couldn't be the real moon
just a trick with mirrors, a mere reflection
you pointed to the sky and said
'It's raining and dark now
and why do the stars look sad if this is not the moon?'

on the way home, with the moon in the boot of the car
you wept, your head on my knee
I asked why you were crying
you who can take the moon from the sky
you said, 'It's raining and dark now
and the stars are sad without the warmth of moonlight.'

a light bulb hangs in the sky in place now
every midsummer by Jacksons pond we make love beneath it
somehow it's just not the same.

Andrew Nash

Days End

Red tinted clouds in a sky deepening blue,
Long shifting shadows a day nearly through.
A blackbird above with his bright piercing eye,
His twilight song fills the darkening sky.

But soon there's a hush as the sun in the west,
Gives a last warming kiss as she sinks down to rest.
And over the earth in the fast failing light,
Mother Nature breaths softly a whispered goodnight.

Michael J McHugh

Someone

Someone to run with and have a laugh
To walk hand in hand along a leafy path
A shoulder to cry on when sadness prevails
Someone to turn to when all else fails
To be gentle and calm most of the time
Yet show anger with only reason and rhyme
To be free as a child enjoying its play
Take nothing for granted, give time to pray
Someone to respect, love and adore
To care and be cared for, who could ask more
Enjoying ones dreams and hopes to share
Stand by through all odds and still be there
Fall flat on ones face with only a sigh
To get up again and reach for the sky
With finger tips to touch, the smile on your face
To be in your arms, what better place
Work all the day and into the night
It's giving and taking all should be right
Life isn't perfect, and people aren't fair
To find the right person in this life, is rare
Someone to be a friend and companion too
All this I believe, that someone is you.

Steve Jackson

Alcoholics a Cure

Where there is no agitation,
      As in low temperature physics,
Change is swift
      And easy.

Instead of feeling
A gut-hole
Sculpted into you,
As if by Henry Moore,

You will discover
An. . . Illicit Still
Where God
Is quietly
Whooping it up.

M J K

Untitled

I wake up in the cold twisted night,
with nothing before me,
but my sight.

I lay in the turmoil of my room,
a victim of shadowy forms,
amorphous threats.

I wake up in the night,
gambling on fixed bets and loaded dice.

The contented dreams of twisted sheets
numbs the pain of grey streets,
and the storm that howls without rain or gale.

The cold slice of scalpel reality is scary,
so scary.
Don't pull me so tightly,
for I'll cling to you,
and let my freedom gush away in the
freedom you give.

Ian Alexander Alty

The Wraith

Summoned by moonlight
She rose from the sod,
Only to seek
To search in vain,
Over crag and crevice
And heather spread heath,

A white wan form
Bereft, forlorn,
Relentlessly driven
Towards the house drawn;
Barred by the window
Banished at the door,
Unable to enter,
Shrouded from life
By the veil of death.

Alone in his room
Her love lies sleeping
Dreaming demented,
Of his former tormentor.

She on the outside
Misses him,
His warm embrace
Strong arm, stern face;

She lingers,
Languishes by the gate
Lamenting her living love,
Selfishly longing for his demise,
Only death can heal the rift
Return Catherine, to her Heathcliff.

Jane B Kearney-Leach

Everest the Hard Way

Dear Everest Double Glazing Windows,
Your panes are as tough as your adverts say.
I tried that test (The one John Noakes shows)
I hired a crane. It arrived last Tuesday
And I swung the steel ball towards the glass
(I'd bet my wife it would withstand the blast)
The ball hit me. (My concussion will pass).
My second swing missed again; sailed right past
Our house, but alas, not next doors' garage
And on the rebound it flattened our cat.
The neighbours started giving a barrage
Of abuse; how dare they swear at me like that.
Your glass survived. Strike three was on target.
Pity our house wasn't built just like it.

Arthur Chappell

A Course of Nature

In the sun's ultraviolet rays
a burly caterpillar crawls,
and constantly lusts for green leaves;
as it consumes it yearns and leaves
a trail like *Achilles' heel,* and
wrath.

A rustic brown corpse; chrysalis.
Dormant; till realisation
of freedom's and *satyrs'* ambition.

Papilio Ulysses: -

Oddysseus your sapphirine sky
wings palpitate freely, to fly
away, high away, in a bright
blaze of white light.

Sweet freedom whispered in my ear -
'You're a butterfly. And butterfly's are free to fly. . .'

Audaye K Elesedy

The Outcast

My family revile me
My friends walk away
I am a social outcast
Rejected more each day.

This crime I have committed?
I do not kill or rape
I do not mug old ladies
Nor property deface.

I cannot go in public places
I cannot go near babies
Yet I am not contagious
Have no scars upon my face.

I'm not a young car stealer
Nor a hardened criminal mind
If I was, perhaps you'd have
Some compassion for my crime.

What is this crime then?
This deed so dire and dread?
I like to light a cigarette,
What's worse I smoke in bed!

Sheila Wicks

Taught by Nature

A silhouette at the water's rim:
flat beak juts from rounded head,
supple neck flows into hollow back,
feathers tuft together as a tail,
the duck waddles left then right,
tilts her head in counterbalance,
her awkward rhythm
a concentrated effort.

Launched chest first
she sails away
easy and graceful
glides across the pool.
Examine her clumsy feet now;
see two efficient paddles
alternating to propel her.
Gifted Mistress of the Marsh.

Pat Livingston

Living on

My voice is the sound of the sunshine,
My presence the kiss of a dream.
I am happiness and tranquillity,
My spirit, the flow of a stream.

Reach out - can you feel me?
I'm with you, I'm here.
I surround you, I touch you,
I am always so near.

Look with your heart - you will see me,
I am warmth, I'm forever, I'm true.
You will hear me when you hear silence,
I am night, I am day, I am you.

I am the past, the present, the future,
I am love, I am peace, I am free.
A hope, a prayer, the song of a child,
I am one, I am all, I am me.

A M Kenyon

Déjà Vu - I Think

Another time, another place
but I do really seem to remember your face
Am I sure, was it you
or is it just a case of déjà-vu?
'I can't quite put my finger on it.'
Perhaps your name might ring a bell
my feelings they tell me I know you quite well
oh well forget it, it doesn't really matter
you'll have to excuse my confusing chatter.

Pauline Jackson

Four O'Clock Club

Here we are again then, at four o'clock in the morning,
Wide awake as usual - and thinking, of course!
We try to plan lucid, witty letters or persuasive telephone calls,
While lawyers and politicians make inspired speeches to the ceiling
And teachers give memorable lessons to the duvet.

But at the top of the agenda is: Worrying.
Family, money, work - those familiar mole-mountains of anxiety
Loom large at four o'clock in the morning.
Seeking solutions we thrash about before moving on
To the Water Passing Ritual. (An item which cannot be deferred.)

Associate Members of The Four O'clock Club, awake beside a sleeper,
Slip quietly out of bed to glide through the dark
And back again with the smug smoothness of practised technique.

Full Members, who sleep alone, can switch on the light, the radio
And the kettle. Then they twitch curtains and peer our
At the comforting patchwork light-shapes - secret symbols of
communication
Between insomniacs who will not recognise each other
When they meet, incognito, for four o'clock afternoon tea.

Meanwhile, apart but forgathered in spirit, the meeting of minds
Continues, despite prolonged interruptions by vociferous, newly arrived
Young Members. Recently enrolled, they have not learnt the rules, unlike
The Seniors, who sometimes resign from Life Membership
Of the Club, at four o'clock in the morning.

Margaret McMichael

Spring in the City

Morning
Hurries up my stairs like a welcome child;
Beams in brass from doorknob and fingerplate,
Beckons me down to glow, for an instant,
In the porch's stained glass heraldry.

Out in the street
I inhale sunlight.
Pale-gold and cool it fills my air - sacs,
Buoyant in my veins like the best wine.
Through the latchings of my lashes I squint at the intensity of blue,
Where white wisps drift and snag on the chimney-pots.
Catkins dangle on a red brick wall.
New green cracks through the paving-stones,
Rosettes and filaments.

In the cemetery
Daffodils proclaim themselves from the grass,
Full-throated and brimming with the sun's yellow,
And under the rich earth, humescent with the gatherings of years,
The bodies of our dead are composted for petals.

Dorothy Ng

Well Remembered

Yes, I remember Fred, or was it Joe?
His Stand lay between the 'Plough'
And the station approach. I remember
Him well! He's dead, you say?

Nice chap, always cheerful. Kept his
Papers tidy and clean. I remember
Ted well. Or was it Jim - or Jack?
Whatever was his name?

Always ready to listen - very polite,
Called you 'Sir,' as he took your change,
Did Ken, or Clem - what was his name?
His face - I remember it well.

He's gone you say? Poor old Sam, or
Dan was it now? I think it was Dan.
Hard to believe he'll sell no more papers
- Now I remember, 'twas Larry! - or Harry.

What was his name? Perhaps it was Les?
No! I really can't say. But I do remember
The face - and the 'Thank you, Sir.'
I've just forgotten the name.

M W Hughes

For Hollie-Claire

Oh, to be the child I used to be!
That which sweet innocence each morning brings,
And on the dancing feet of life,
Sends her forth into the day on eager wings.

Her hair like corn and tender satin skin,
Her slow sweet smile that winds around my heart,
And when unsure, her little trusting hand,
Which softly slips in mine as teardrops start.

Her childish laughter by a sparkling brook,
Which, chuckling too, embraces eager hands,
Her flying limbs through clover studded fields,
And tiny footprints etched in tide-wet sands.

Too soon she hovers on the brink -
- of childhood, and the days fly past,
Whilst I with yearning must look on,
Must snatch at time and try to hold it fast.

Oh, why do cherished hours so quickly flee,
And leave sweet memories fondly tucked away,
The years roll by, departing every one,
Now adult troubles banish simple play.

But now my own small child recalls each dream,
And life itself is dearer now to me,
For through her bright and shining eyes,
I see once more the child I used to be.

June Field

Memory

Brown cracked leather prickles my legs.
Fat and hard, the arm of the couch
pushes at my back.
Soft and baby-bathed, powdery-scented,
I twine blue ribbon through fat digits,
pull frayed edges to my lips,
feel the smoothness on my cheek.
       I'm vulnerable.
Grandad, swooping down,
lifts me high
twirls me round.
Windows, furniture, doors, carousel.
Crinkly skin, whiskery chin,
white hair gripped by stubby fingers.
Blue eyes twinkling
shine love into my small self.
Rhythm of 'Housewives' Choice'
radio's a living-room polka.
Long white dress flows and sparkles,
catches light in meandering folds.
Tweedy roughness thrills bare legs.

An arm hooked round the dry-warm neck
I lean from wide supportive shoulders
to point to mother, grandmother
spinning past our heady dance.
I laugh and breathe tobacco pipe smell.
I love Grandad.

Infant security focused in a moment,
lives with me, holds me,
forty years on, though Grandad's long, long, gone.
Happy chance for me to be his daughter's child.

Hilary Tinsley

November

Who says November is always so dull,
It can be alive with colour and light
When fells are clothed in russet and yellow,
With stiff crunchy bracken and crisp beech leaves.
Where becks sparkle down all silver and white
Into the limpid blue calm of the lakes.
The slender soft grace of the larch trees
Stands clear on a sunlit hillside.

The gentle green roll of the foothills
Seems to rise in a series of curves.
It dips to a fold as a new hill begins.
There's a tumble of rocks on the skyline
Tow'ring in peaks like the lion and the lamb.
Then down sweeps a mist to hide all the tops.
On the lower slopes though, the sun still shines
On Loughrigg Fell.

Down on the shore, the lake, like a mirror
Reflects the details of colour and shapes.
In reverse we see the russet and gold:
The top of Nab Scar; the cottage below;
The tumbling beck and the larch trees grace.
The swan, seeing its image, looks down in
Wonder, on Rydal now.

We saunter beside the Rothay's green bank.
A small dark bird flits over the river.
Now it is running on rocks 'neath the stream.
With a bib so white - a dipper surely.
The water ousel. 'Ah: there goes its mate.'
How lovely the gulls look, whirling, calling,
Round the island today.

Violet May Eastham

Variation on Shakespeare's Sonnet
(Written for my husband, Mike on our Wedding Anniversary)

Shall I compare thee to a fine red wine,
Smooth poured from out its crystal flask,
Bounteous fruits plucked off the vine,
With love, kept safe, in oaken casks?
Secreted, stored, for testing time,
Matured in peaceful, airy gloom.
Full bodied, rich, delicious, fine,
A tasty glass, or two, consumed?
But unlike love, wine cannot breathe
Love lives, entwines and is divine
Cause hearts to leap, be worn on sleeves,
Entwined, forever, yours and mine,
Until that day life ebbs from me
In love, devoted I shall be.

Betty Lightfoot

This Creature Insanity

Insanity has me walking round,
looking for a place which can't be found.
Following footsteps in the snow,
It's my only sign of where to go.
The footsteps end outside the door,
on to the edge, stepped once before,
déjà vu strikes once again,
past and present in my brain.

The creature from below,
decided he would show.
He hasn't come to entertain,
he's come to drive us all insane.
I'm sure that he'll succeed,
our eyes, our nose, our ears bleed.
Causing chaos and frustration,
doesn't hold out compensation.
Come to destroy,
come to annoy,
come to collect, inspect,
detect, reject,
clawing at our intellect.

Under the bridge,
the creature does hide.
He stalks the night for genocide.
Not one or two his soul will take,
but a thousand, a million are in his wake.
Venture not into the night,
lock all your doors,
turn out the lights.
Don't make a sound,
suffer in silence,
protect yourself from insanic violence.

In the ghettos grown men shiver.
Drive the car down to the river.
Leave off the brakes and drive it in,
knowing that you cannot swim.
Oozing out plasmic fornication,
can't relate to meditation,
stimulate your mental state,
hallucinate your very own fate,
How - will - you - die?

Mark Hughes

The Alien

self
assembled
after
sleep
down
the
stairs
across
the
floor

all
that
nearly
made
a
man
burst
through
his
own
front
door

and
scattered
down
the
garden
path
and
flapped
against
the
fence

bits
they
almost
recognised
and
things
that
made
no
sense

S Brady

A Smile

It only takes a moment to give a little smile
Then you will find you'll get one back
It really is worthwhile
It only takes a moment to smile your cares away
Then you will find to your surprise
You'll have a happier day
A face can be so beautiful when lit up with a smile
It's better than a gloomy one that makes you run a mile
So always try regardless, a funny smile will do
As long as you are smiling, the sun will shine for you.

Hilde Leary

Rosary Beads

Rosary beads pass slowly
Through delicate fingers
Whispered prayers skip sibilantly
From pursed and nervous lips
Eyes, which see it all
Grasp vague images of hope,
In torment.

And there she sat for hours
Until the cool night came and
Buried her, bit by bit.
She was lost, confused,
Afraid, consumed.

Rosary beads pass slowly
Through delicate fingers
A soft and silent procession
In honour of mortal despair
Still, that taste hangs upon the air
Like candleflame, bitter and slain.
Irreverent doubt.

David Ray

I Wonder Why?

When she was nine
my friend saw
a dead man
with staring eyes
and an open mouth,
hanging,
in an old, wooden shed,
in a yard.
He wore his best suit
and his curled fingers
carefully held down
the hem
of his jacket.
I wonder why?

Denise Southern

Utah Beach
(Normandy D-Day 1945)

As I came and looked in awe
to where bombs fell
and blood did pour,
where sky was red
which lit the dead
the guns had left
to rest in peace
hearts beat no more
the toll of war.
Men ran like ants
no time for fear,
the blood was shed
as death drew near.
The foe at flanks
scanned rows of tanks,
then the long wait
men stood as bait.
Cries of the sane
rang out in pain,
as men were slain
war has no gain.
Now the old
count the cost,
of young lives lost.
So brave and bold
as those loud guns
killed death's young sons.

Sally March

Easy Street

Walking down your road,
Seeing beauty in the pavement stars,
Becoming a part in the lamplit aura of the terrace,
With its rushing drains and sleeping melodrama.
Outstaring the cats,
Frozen for a moment in disbelief
At this intrusion into their nocturnal scene.

The day was yours,
The night is all mine,
For even the drunkards have lurched
In the direction of somewhere,
To remind them of their lives.
And I am left, under a washed out moon,
walking between the hundreds,
Behind their walls, their bricked-up senselessness.

Now it is easy to feel alone;
No irritation to deceive me,
To distract me from the ache
Of a soul hollowed out by time.

David Sharpe

Refugees

Though we recognise the pattern of existence
that makes stark skeletons
of all our beasts and beds, our fruit trees and our farms,

That drove us out upon the roads with ragged bundles
to fill the gap
which formerly lay between the rearguards and the vanguards,

To become an accepted target for relief appeals,
watched over enigmatically
by figures with blue helmets in chattering armoured cars.

We are not entirely satisfied
of the happiness
of the casual mound or communal grave.

We are not entirely satisfied
of the fortune of those
from amongst us who occupy or share them.

In the ditches and barns and camps we are quietly breeding
and each birth amongst us
poses again the prospect of hope for a while.

For we accept the misery, knowing our children
will be settled,
strong-limbed, fertile and quickly forgetting.

We accept also this pattern which permits some future generation,
patient and soil-rooted,
to be driven out again upon the roads,

Again to suffer the misery, the wasted limbs and the bundles,
again to distrust death,
again to endure the sweet hopes of the quiet, public breeding.

Jack Butler

A World in Need of Peace and Help

Somalia's starving small ones sitting in the sun,
Food flying fast to fearing folk.
Moss Side murders getting more and more,
Dead bodies lying on the floor,
No need for numerous bullet proof vests.
Romania's reeking orphanages,
Trained helpers cuddling, loving.
IRA send bombs blowing,
People dying, relatives crying,
Folks feeling friendly, friendship.
Children of Brazil crying,
In the sewers living, dying,
Parents loving, caring, adopting,
All the children living properly.
Racial rows running on,
Where's peace there?

Sarah Lamb (10)

Conquistador

Conquistador, can you explain
your tactics in The Grand Campaign?
The artful way you scheme attacks?
The moves you make to hide your tracks?
Oh warrior bold, where did you train?

Old bills you keep for 'Free Champagne'
with lists of names to 'Entertain',
here pencilled in your filofax,
Conquistador.

Shivering on a barren plain,
pale refugees wait in the rain;
they've swapped their gloves and anoraks,
their savings from the Halifax
for brochure homes in sunny Spain.
Con-quistador!

Pennant Roberts

Life's Cycle

The Baby Boy
with bright blue eyes,
with fluffy down, sparse round his ears,
flays chubby hands around his cot
reaching for the sky.
Burbles out unwanted feed, through pinkish gums
devoid of teeth.
Untouched by time - his cares are few.
He's one week old - *Life is New.*

The Old Man
Has pale blue eyes, now dimmed with age.
Has wisps of grey around his crown.
He stretches out the vein etched hands
towards a distant shore - he dribbles slaver, as
a toothless grin widens his lips.
The years fall from his feeble frame
the pain-racked face grows smooth and calm.
Beyond his room, a skylark sings,
he splutters twice - *New Life Begins.*

Eadie Logan

The Salt Flats

The sheep and the salt flats don't mix; you can tell.
Passing them, aloof, in an embankmented summer train,
The scattered wayward flock are down there, busy
Wolfing-up the sparse salty patches of sea grass
In-between the slippery, steep-sided gullies
That meander out towards low tide.

But they're only half-animals. . . far and away
Too light for their average agricultural genre.
Their sun-parched, mud-caked, entwined strands
Of fly-buzzed wool ruffling
In the constant sea breeze as they stand:
In rapt catatonia, semi-emaciated - almost ready
For the crows to peck at.

Overhead
In tiny, sinister, reverse polka dot silhouette,
The bustling carrion circle and caw, impatiently
Watching, waiting, for a careless step. Not even
Brief, nonchalant glances between gulps, down
At a gaunt, white, horned, sand-embedded skull
(An ex-close-knit family member?)
Gaping up from a wet gully bottom in grim, hollow testament
Disturbs the fold's mammoth indifference, their spectacular
Shortsightedness.

They should be well out of it, frisking
Upon a fresher, sweeter fare,
Upon lush, dew-laden, skylarked meadows and
Acquiring a good sun tan.
But no, they're beyond advice - preoccupied -
Biting, munching, staring, sleeping.

The people and the city don't mix. . .
Michael Lakey

191

Who Made the Broken Hearted Babe

So this is what they call my world what they call my life
Brought forth innocent
From the dreamy other world of my mother's womb
It cost no money to feed me.
As long as my heart beat they'd keep me
Into the light the sanctified wish of husband and wife
They just left it to God to watch over me
For just a few moments the warmth of her breast
Then snatched away she must have her rest
But already planning what could be done
With the human milk wasting as from her nipple it ran
He will get big and get fat I'm sure about that
Just as well on an artificial diet. Buy a packet and try it.
My voice cried out I want love and devotion
But she was in her world of afterbirth pain
Her passion and her compassion wrapped up in emotion
She thought she was the one who carried the can.
I am here and here's where I am.
I looked at my father and he looked at me.
What do we do now? Hope it isn't a she.
He held my hand. Yes, he looks like you.
Will he make that claim, will he do the same when I'm twenty-two?
He'd planned to buy a brand new car
But now I was here things would stay as they are.
The rising mortgage for mortar and bricks.
No more night life. No more spending money just for the kicks.
Oh God, if you are in the sky hear my cry and dry my eye
There are three hearts here, make them one
And may the warmth of our laughter
Dry up the spring that are tears.

Gertrude Worrall

Funny you Feel it too

We're living in a bad dream
Never understood others and superstitions
Then I realise it's only a condition
Life itself, there in high esteem.

When my thoughts struggle in the night
There seems to be a confusion
Under all this illusion
Mister Moon's a star in his own right
And me a scar in his own blight
Why do I have to suffer yesterday and days gone by.

The summer of love may have ended with a dying fall
But no one kills a dreamer
Here comes the leaders of tomorrow and the losers of today
And there's nothing we can do.

Closing both eyes your head filled with light
While you are trying to steel the day
All your loves reflected back to you
Not knowing what new day may bring
Where there is nothing left to spare
Something that's never changing
Smiling that's never ageing.

The guiding light in all your love shines on
Eyes that shine from depths of your soul
Fixed by their charm
Those ideas take my control
Funny you feel it too? Like I knew it should
Breathe it always when it's new
And all your love's reflected back to you.

R P Chapman

Visions

Awake within my minds dream
Exploring realities
Only I could create.
Spirits play free
While the physical rests
Surroundings change
Within a moments thought.
A trip around the world
A trip around the universe
Travel further still
Within a mind filled with excitement
Unlimited imagination
Cut loose upon a breeze
Of invisible colours.
Episodes of past
Possibilities of future
Silent screams deafening to hear
Stunned in motion
Dangling arms, dangling legs,
Visions, Visions, Visions.

Geoff Ackers

Thoughts at the Start of the Year

January,
The New Year,
Still wearing its baby booties,
Lies crooning in its cradle.
What lies ahead, on that blank page
As yet unmarked by daily scribblings.
The New Year,
It's smile full of promise,
It's a happy gurgling full of hope.

March,
And the year, still young,
Gambols with spring lambs
In flower-strewn meadows.
Why waste her youthful energy
In squabbling over who first saw the caterpillar,
When together, we can watch
The emerging butterfly
Spread her rainbow wings
To dry in the warm sunshine.

July,
The year, now at the height of her powers,
Spends her longest days
Working hard to fulfil the promise
Of her spring blossoms.
Now is the time she labours
To turn her hopes into realities.

September,
The year, now full-blown
And full of blowsy generosity,
Pours out her ample harvest,
But what of her twin children,
Hope and promise?
Do they run on rounded sun-tanned legs,
Or do they limp,
Sickly and undernourished?

December,
The year, now frail and fading fast,
Draws her shawl closer,
And rocks slowly in her chair.
Is she lined and drawn,
Her face soured with might-have-beens?
Or does she sit, with twinkling eyes,
Smiling on her progeny,
Chuckling to herself at her memories?

So, come little January,
There's a long way to go.
Put on your bonnet, hold my hand,
And we'll travel on together!

Veronica Jackson

For Those Who Have Fought and Died

Dread the dead oh veils of awe,
revere the fear of perils jaw.

Hideous are the myriad's of battles
never asking *Why?*

Those born as innocents should be
chosen to die.

No movements, no senses, no sound
from the braves.

Terrible the white stones
so silent
the grass graves.

D Dealy

Three Gripes

A Parliamentary Riot
We've had a parliamentary riot.
Madam speaker couldn't keep 'em quiet.
When it was announced that they must,
Like industry going bust,
Agree that their numbers be lessened.
'Oh no,' said MP's.
'Oh, please, Madame, please
We can't be ruined by this cruel disease.'

Redundancy Money
'Our firm is going bust,' they said,
Slowly running out of bread.
Redundancy the only offer.
Hell. . . they don't deal in copper
They gave me fifty grand.
Come join the wagon with a band.

Not Twice Gazuped
Estate agent, Jones by name,
Said, 'I am not to blame,
If your house won't sell.'
You gazumped us when we bought,' said Ken,
'The price went up at least by ten,
We'll won't be cheated now as well.'

Jack Whitaker

Wasp

menaced horror of your sudden flight
unprovoked behaviour, gang mentality
wearing town colours
acid yellow, absorbed black
bone vibrated wings stir sultry air
and brush against down covered cheek
with lover's lightest touch

two curved probes stroke the surface
mouth parts suck pearled liquid where
soft flesh spurts through sliced skin
breaks nets of clotted healing
to oozing maiden juice within
the pulsed rear taps, retracts in ecstasy
commits the rape.

Carole Carr

When Eyes No Longer See

Tho' the windows of life can no longer see
The flush of the dawn that paints with rose
The sleeping fields and the silent town;

Tho' the wondering look in a baby's eyes
Is just a remembered thing
I feel no sadness, I have my thoughts
And memories sharp that a name can bring
Into my mind as days pass by,
While I sit and wonder how things have changed,
And whether the scenes that I recall
Do in fact remain at all.

Is it a pleasure, or is it a pain
Not knowing what memories still remain
Just as they were in days gone by
When vision was a natural gift
And thoughts of loss did not occur?

When blossoming spring was taken for granted,
When sparkling summer and autumn's fire
Were not really recorded except by desire
To spend the days in leisurely style,
To ignore the chill of winter awhile.

But the time has gone, the blinds are drawn;
I don't see the glow of early dawn;
The sun can't guide me thru' the day
Since, like daylight, my sight went away.

Leslie Woods

Out of the Depths

I am a ghost from the suffering Third World;
I died of starvation and need,
Yet now, as I roam through this vast universe,
I'm appalled by the waste and the greed;
By all the indifference to hunger and pain;
The couldn't care less point of view;
You can't comprehend the depth of despair
That the sight of all this drives me to!

Two thirds of the world live in misery and want,
In ignorance, sickness and fear;
Bedevilled by earthquake or famine and flood
Their existence is made yet more drear.
No hope of a future, they live day to day;
In hope of survival they toil;
E'en then, oft exploited by tariffs and tax
Are the fruits of their labour and soil.

One third of the world in affluence lives,
Uncaring and quite unaware
Of the great moral outrage they help perpetrate
By accepting this unequal share
Of all life's essentials, it's comforts and gains
Made at the expense of the lost;
As rich grow much richer whilst poor get more poor,
I dread the inevitable cost!

I beg your assistance to help remedy
This shameful, inhuman affair,
By fighting the cause of the piteous Third World
And bringing more pressure to bear
On leaders and peoples for greater support,
On industries for to impart
Their knowledge and techniques into these poor lands,
Thus giving my people some heart

And reason to hope that they too might enjoy
A lifetime of prosperity,
Instead of believing that, e're they've grown old,
They'll land in their cold graves, like me!
So please, I entreat you, do hearken my plea
And answer my earnest request,
For then, only then, will my mission be o'er
And I can then lay me to rest.

Mary P Lucas

The Beginning and the End

The old man's face is lined and wrinkled
his hair is streaked with grey,
The hands that lay upon his lap are
cracked like lumps of clay,
Yet he has lived, he knows what life
is all about,
For he has tasted bitterness, love,
happiness and strife.

The young boy standing at his side
with skin so soft and tender,
Knows nothing of the ways of life,
the love, the hate, the splendour,
He has his life ahead of him, he's
only just begun,
Will it be a happy one, with wisdom,
love and fun.

The old man and the young boy, a
Grandad and Grandson,
The little boy so innocent, the other
worldly wise,
Packing all he can into his life before
he dies,
And if he died tomorrow, I know the
things he'd like to say,
Enjoy your life, live to the full
Oh yes, I've had my day.

Allison Magee

Gloomy Tuesday

Murky day
Drizzle splatters
Wind blowing through
Archways

Heads bowed down
Umbrellas inside out
In the city square

Rain soaked pavements
Shops displaying
To an empty audience

Gloomy Tuesday
You've come, round again
On this January day

Rain hammers of
Taxis, parked up
Waiting for a fare

Engines running
Heaters on
Windows shut
Keeping warm

Gloomy Tuesday
Sky grey
Storm clouds, here we go
Rain again

Gloomy Tuesday
I wish you'd go away

H Chmielechi

On Castle Crag

On a small hill it was,
Dwarfed by a looming mountain
That lay, haloed in cloud
Like a sleeping beast.
In a dip at its top,
Hemmed in by trees resting deftly
On cracked, broken crags
Where glass-eyed sheep stare,
There stood a huge boulder, upended
As if flung from the sky in anger.

A dead weight it was, unmoving
Towering six or seven feet
And heavy like a clenched fist,
A granite altar to all of earth's
Lifeless, unyielding things.

Yet from top to bottom
This stone was split,
Rock splintered from rock
Like a shattered fragile shell,
And through the gap a sapling
Stretched skyward,
Splitting brute weight
It surged upward towards light
Like a man bursting from water.

Was it a kind of birth then?
A quiet, heaving birth obscure,
Unseen in the silence of those drizzling hills,
A straining from darkness,
From nothing
Into life's pulsating air.
And it was as if I could hear
The rhythmic whirr of awakening,
The crisp unwinding of leaf and branch
Sucked upward and out
By the driving light of life,
And saw life's secret struggle
In a cloudy silent land.

Mark Murphy

John Parker Square SW11 - 3rd January 1993

Today reality wrenched my mind
and forced me to meet it eye to eye.

A sudden call by telephone
quenched all my calm,
and spawned a clutch of nightmares
with unbridled ease.

A knife at night:
and my own son
was chosen as a stranger's prey.

A mother's bonds,
no matter if they're loosely tied,
are oxen strong.

The hour I heard,
I suffered cliché's Little Death.
My faltering spirit guttered,
damped,
within a vacuum of fear.

I offer thanks that he escaped
with life intact,
though not unscathed:
and pray to never feel again
the brain and limb dissolving shock
that froze my guts
and snatched the simplest thoughts away
beyond my power to frame.

I summoned only strength to shun
the fatal words
'What if. . .?'
Freda Bunce

Unheard

Between the oaks, church clock doth peep
And speaks the hour in dulcet chime
But not to those in plots who sleep
Ears deaf for eternal time
Once they loved to hear
The church's organ strains
To weddings that began
In English country lanes
No more cries from lips of cherubs
Doused in holy water
Can those ears detect
Be they son or daughter
So ring out church bells
With peals of joy and laughter
Better we do hear it now
Than never in hereafter

Anthony Rupert Bland

Romantic Love

There was once a day, in May,
In my youth, when sunshine
Bathed the fields with a richness
of sweet delicacy.

And freshly cut grass in the park
Perfumed the air exquisitely;
And the sunset that night in May
Coloured pink and mauve and crimson
The whitewashed cottages of the village.

The air cooled as we walked across the bridge
of happiness - full of delight and the
Romantic love of springtime,
Quite unable to wait for old moon and the
Silver shafts of starlight.

Memories of the day, warm and tucked away
within us, lay secure in the bosom of our young lives,
No-one else allowed to touch them or sully
their precious secret place.

Our love:- spiritual and all-enveloping, moved towards
The inn with carpets-red, and hearth of fiery stone.
My hand, on your right hip, fell away to close
The portal'd door.

Alcohol warmed the very tips of toes and fingers,
Mateus Rosé' glinted in the firelight;
The shape of the bottle pleased my hand -
Like a breast.
Desire, and warmth, and all-consuming dreams.

Howard Procter

However

If there's one word that drives me to the end of my tether
Then it's that word of disappointment and rejection... *However*
It crops up everywhere, its so totally absurd
But never underestimate the power of this adverb
So why do I detest it, its uses are ample?
Well let me give a clue with the following example...

Thank you for your job application... *However*, at this present time...
Right Sir, you've finished your driving test... *However*, about that 'One-
Way' sign...
This is your Captain speaking, welcome aboard... *However*, due to fog...
Merry Christmas from all at number twenty-seven... *However*, if *your*
dog...
To-day will start warm, dry and sunny... *However*, by late afternoon...
We received your Insurance claim sir... *However*, under the heading of
'Sonic Boom...'
Yes, you *can* pay by credit card... *However*, due to the date of expiry...
The winner of the two-thirty is number six... *However*, after a steward's
enquiry...
We are pleased to offer you a loan Sir... *However*, there is a limit on what
we lend...
I was flattered by your poem and yes I *do* like you... *However*, only as a
friend...
We hope you enjoyed to-night's programme... *However*, next week's
edition...
Our Surveyor values your house at fifty-thousand... *However*, due to a
suspicion...
I can confirm your rights to property Sir... *However*, one of your family's
descendants...
Welcome to the hotel Senor... *However*, due to building amendments...

So now you see why this word always gives me the blues
Its because the words that follow... *However*... usually bring bad news!

Simon C Allison

So Sorry Mother

In infancy we nestled in her tender loving care.
As children we'd rush home from school and she was always there.
That's why what we've done to her is very hard to bear:
We've put her in a home!

In the recession of the 30's and no work for our Dad
she'd go without to feed us and give us all she had.
So you will understand that we were very very sad
To put her in a home!

Our children really loved their Gran and when they went to stay,
they'd enter into Fairyland with happiness all day;
Somewhere where they'd love to be and never come away.
But now she's in a home!

She had a stroke, she couldn't walk, at home she would have died.
We just couldn't manage her no matter how we tried.
Then the Doctors and the Nurses on whom we'd all relied
said *'Put her in a home!'*

The surroundings they are perfect, she's cared for and well fed.
She sits and sleeps and eats and chats and then she goes to bed.
So is it quite so awful, the place that we all dread,
A safe and caring home?

Margaret Swaffer

Sonnet to a Pessimistic Friend

Shall I compare thee to a winter's day?
Thou art more wet, and much more miserable.
And when we see those darling buds of May
You may cheer up, but yet I doubt it, mate.
You look at all the darker sides of things.
You never count your blessings every one.
You wish that you were rich and idle: when
The silver linings you would look upon.
Not so; should you inherit millions without end,
Scrooge like you'd hoard them, being much afraid
That folk would like you only when you'd spend.
So thinking, more unhappy you would then become.
So long we live on this our planet, chum
So long, but seeming longer when we're glum.

K Farley

Recuperation in Dorset

I have seen the morning sun come up
and make the grey mists go,
and paint each house and cottage
with its warm and special glow.

I have trodden soft and yielding sand
where sea and shoreline meet,
and found imprints of age-old leaves
and prehistoric feet.

I have felt the awe of towering rocks
and thrilled to the Dorset scene:
I have known the joy of new-found friends
who pursued a kindred theme.

I've sensed the spanning centuries
which link so much I've seen,
and feel I've built my memories
in a celestial time-machine.

Not least, I found awareness
that life's not just flat and grey -
but needs an inner prompting
to find highlights every day.

P C Kippax

Sunday Archaeologist

'Remind me not to put my fingers in my mouth.'
He's picking shards like loosened teeth,
The biscuit brown, the blue, the white, the blue and white.
The shallow stream smells sickly sweet,
Leaching rain from clinker beds
Beneath the twitch-grass, dock and reeds,
What's left of all our parents' fires.
We're treading on their hearths' desires.

David Langston

Salford
Madness
Community
Church

If I was the vicar
of this church
the first thing
I'd do is take
down the sign
that says:
No right of way
to public
No cycling
I'd invite the kids
down to spray
paint the walls
I'd stick up a
notice that said:
Public right of way
Cyclists welcome
punctures repaired
But perhaps there's
a method in their
madness after all

Danny Wise

Picnic

A bird's call
like a phone purring softly.

The side of the hill
massaged by light
glows, but the crest
is hooded.

We picnic
in an island
of napkins and cups.

The grass has left
green crayon
on my palms.

Leaves' gold wings
lie around us.
They've been stripped
by wind.

Shadows are soft pencil-strokes
on the spread cloth.

If children were here
they'd touch the tamarisk.

But we're grown-up,
taking a break,
fondling ourselves.
The cups clatter.

The bird stops ringing.

William Park

Where am I?

Dark.
Through the slow, rising, awareness of my disembodied eyes
I ooze into consciousness.
(If I am aware of the blackness of nothing, surely I must be
Alive and awake?)

Still.
I am only eyes and brain
There is nothing else
Until the dawn, or I move
Becoming conscious of my body
Only by the changing texture of the bedclothes.

Strange.
This is not my bed.
The atmosphere feels foreign, unfamiliar, disorienting
I don't know where I am -
And then the gradual remembrance
Of booking into the hotel last night
Focuses its image in my head.

Quiet.
Thoughts roaming free in the silence
And I wonder,
If I can come to some agreement with life
Maybe give up my endless questioning
In return for just a little understanding
Of what it is about.

But perhaps it isn't about or for anything -
Anyway, it doesn't seem to want
To make any bargains
And it always has the last word.

John Tickner

Kipling I Miss you

O Rudyard, Rudyard, come ye back
Your absence is lamented.
To read insipid poems and stories
And sit back discontented.
No thrilling plots of Raj and Queen
No Kim or Gungadin.
No Indian summer to warm the winter
And make my blood run thin.
Your thoughts, your words, your Mandalayan soul
I cherish every page
I smell the spices, I feel I'm there,
For this was Kiplings' age.

Edward Ellis Doyle

Outrage
(In memory of James Bulger, died February 1993)

Bad news travels fast they say
The cloud spreads o'er the city
Creating evil in men's minds
No love, only pity.

Pity and hatred in men's hearts
For now the deed is done
Panic spreads like wildfire
Distrust and fear are one.

Suspicion of thy neighbour, friend,
Clouds the starless skies,
Despair and anger everywhere
Seed of Sodom multiplies.

Daylight hours are filled with fear
Night brings only cries.
Heartbreak seeps through a city
When a child dies.

Jean Carroll

St Helens 1

The breezes which bring the dusts of roadworks
and shimmering locusts of silica
and red lead from landfills
make the already asthmatic
grey sky more deadly -
another burning mucal morning
and death to the chance
of a gulp of clean air.

Seventeen horizon blighting
chimneys are belching
and I'll still have to go for a run -
to rest would only hasten my decline.

Stephen Kenny

The Ghosts of Lullingstone Villa

Hide and seek on summer days
When we were young - carefree,
We thought such days would have to end,
How wrong one's thoughts can be.

When autumn came your legion marched
To fight the northern foe,
I wept and felt my heart would break
And could not watch you go.

A cold, cold winter lingered on,
For you I sadly yearned.
One icy day a shout went up.
'The legion is returned.'

But it was in the spring before
We saw our men again,
Sad shadows moving t'wards us
Through the misty morning rain.

I found you Lucius, gaunt and pale
With death stamped on your brow.
'No more will we be parted.'
I made, right then, that solemn vow.

As slowly life slipped from you
I offered you the phial.
Remember how you smiled at me?
You knew I'd join you in a while.

Now Lucius, I'm going to hide,
Oh how I love this game.
We've played it o'er a thousand years,
Our summer days are here again.
K Sheil